# WINSTON CHURCHILL

# MOLLIE KELLER

# WINSTON CHURCHILL

FRANKLIN WATTS
NEW YORK I LONDON I TORONTO I SYDNEY I 1984
AN IMPACT BIOGRAPHY

A GROLIER COMPANY

Photographs courtesy of: The Bettmann Archive Inc.: pp. 8, 36, 92;
Winston Churchill Memorial Library, Westminster College: p. 23;
Culver Pictures, Inc.: pp. 52, 63, 76, 87, 104; UPI: p. 95.

Library of Congress Cataloging in Publication Data

Keller, Mollie.
Winston Churchill.

(An Impact biography)
Bibliography: p.
Includes index.
Summary: A biography of an outstanding English leader from his
childhood through his years as a statesman and prime minister.
1. Churchill, Winston, Sir, 1874-1965—Juvenile
literature. 2. Great Britain—Politics and government—
20th century—Juvenile literature. 3. Great Britain—
Foreign relations—1936-1945—Juvenile literature.
4. Prime ministers—Great Britain—Biography—Juvenile
literature. [1. Churchill, Winston, Sir, 1874-1965.
2. Prime ministers] I. Title.
DA566.9.C5K44  1984   941.082′092′4 [B] [92] 83-21896
ISBN 0-531-04752-0

# CONTENTS

"I was a child of the Victorian era,
when the structure of our country seemed
firmly set, when its position in trade
and on the seas was unrivalled, when
the realization of the greatness of
our Empire and of our duty to preserve
it was ever growing stronger."

WINSTON CHURCHILL
*A Roving Commission*

# SCHOOLBOY

# 1

No one expected him so soon.

They'd all been told he'd be coming in January, so there seemed to be nothing wrong with taking a holiday in the country. Fresh air, perhaps a little hunting or riding, and a small dinner party or two would be a welcome break from all the planning and waiting.

But Winston Leonard Spencer-Churchill was tired of waiting. Impatient to get on with the business of life, he joined his parents' vacation at Blenheim Palace early in the morning of November 30, 1874. So unexpected was his arrival that a cradle and clothing—even diapers—had to be borrowed from the wife of a local lawyer.

His early arrival was actually a boon to his parents. The London social season would not pick up again until the new year, and by then his mother would have both her strength and her shape back. She was, after all, only twenty years old, and she didn't want to give up one more party or ball than she had to.

For Winston's parents were no ordinary young couple. They were Lord and Lady Randolph Churchill. Randolph, a slender man with popeyes and a walrus mustache, was the youngest son of the Duke of Marlborough. Raised in the same palace his son would be born in, educated at Eton and Oxford, Randolph moved easily and proudly among the leaders of English society. Lady Randolph had been born Jennie Jerome in Brooklyn, New York. The daughter of a New York stockbroker, she'd enjoyed the advantages of American high society as a young girl and had spent her teen-age years at the court of Napoleon III in Paris. During the Franco-Prussian War, Jennie's family moved to the safety of England, where they fit right into the circle that moved around the Prince of Wales. It was, in fact, at one of the prince's balls that Randolph met Jennie. Within three days they were engaged.

Their decision to marry was not greeted with universal approval. Both sets of parents were alarmed at the suddenness of their decision. And while Jennie's parents were pleased that she was marrying into the aristocracy, the duke and duchess were dismayed at their son's choice of an American. They urged the pair to wait a year or at least until Randolph had been elected to Parliament.

Taking them at their word, as soon as the elections of February 1874 had made Randolph a new Member of Parliament, he set the lawyers to work on the elaborate financial contracts that preceded every wealthy marriage. The young lovers were wed in Paris the following April.

Exactly seven and one-half months later Winston was born. Having done her duty and produced a male heir, Jennie went back to her hunting and partying; Randolph went back to the House of Commons. The baby, small, dark, and "wonderfully pretty," as his father noted, was given to the care of a professional nurse, as were all upper-class children of the time.

Mrs. Everest, Winston's nanny, did all the hard work of mothering. She fed him, washed him, changed his diapers, spanked him when he strayed, and cuddled him when he had nightmares. She also watched him take his first steps and heard him speak his first words. She had no other duties but to care for him, and Winston was constantly with her. He called her "Woom" and "Woomany" for to him she was womanhood. Jennie, the only other woman in his life, saw him only on Mrs. Everest's days off and during brief visits with her specially cleaned and dressed son. As he later wrote of his mother: "She shone for me like the evening star. I loved her dearly, but at a distance." It was dear old Woom he relied on for love and comfort until her death.

The year after Winston's birth Randolph meddled in a scandalous divorce case and managed to offend both Queen Victoria and the Prince of Wales. The Churchills were no longer invited anywhere, nor were their invitations accepted, for fear of further distressing the royal family. To save the family honor, the Duke of Marlborough accepted the post of viceroy of Ireland, taking his son to serve as his secretary until the storm blew over. Their exile lasted five years.

Winston's first memories were of Dublin. He recalled the Viceregal Lodge, long, low, and white, surrounded by acres of lawn and entirely ringed by forest. (Revisiting the place as a young man, he was astonished to find that the lawn was about sixty yards from end to end and that the deep forest was well-kept shrubbery.) He didn't spend much time with his parents. Winston saw his mother either in her tight-fitting riding outfit, mud-spattered from a hunt, or rustling through the hall in her evening gown, the large diamond star ornament she loved set in her thick, dark hair. He saw even less of his father. The official documents that arrived daily at the viceroy's office kept him too busy to spend the odd hour in the nursery with his son. Winston's days passed with walks in Phoenix Park to watch the soldiers drill, with rides on his donkey in the garden, and with rare visits to parties, plays, and pantomimes.

Winston's life changed abruptly when his parents decided it was time for him to be educated and engaged a governess to guide his intellectual development. Poor Winston. No longer could he spend the afternoon with his toy steam engine or his tin soldiers, Mrs. Everest sitting close by to answer his questions or join his games. In fact, the very day after Winston learned the dreadful news, Mrs. Everest, whom he had thought would protect him from the governess, produced a little book called *Reading Without Tears*. "It certainly did not justify its title in my case," he later admitted. Everyday he and his nanny would sit down with the book, she pointing her finger at the letters as Winston named them one by one.

But any hopes the unwilling scholar may have had that once he had mastered the alphabet he would be allowed to rejoin his troops were dashed when the governess moved in. Not content to torment him with words and letters, she had another, more wicked torture in her repertoire: arithmetic. Winston, who had to be "sufficiently pressed" to say his letters, baulked at numbers. They were

> tied into all sorts of tangles and did things to one
> another which it was extremely difficult to forecast
> with complete accuracy. You had to say what they
> did each time they were tied up together, and the
> Governess apparently attached great importance
> to the answer being exact. If it was not right, it was
> wrong. It was not any use being "nearly right."

Incensed at such impositions on his time, the 5-year-old Winston went to his mother to plead his case. To his dismay, she sided with the governess.

Politics brought the Churchills back to England. The next general election turned the Conservative Party out of power. The new prime minister, chosen from the victorious Liberal Party, had his own candidate for viceroy of Ireland, and the duke happily returned to Blenheim.

Randolph, who had been reelected, returned to Parliament as a member of Her Majesty's Loyal Opposition. Now part of the minority party, he believed it was his duty to criticize, not to formulate, policy, and became a professional gadfly. Nor was it only the Liberals who felt the sting of his tongue. With several of his friends he formed a splinter group within the Conservative ranks dedicated to the principles of their newly minted "Tory Democracy"—a plan to make upper-class conservatism relevant to the laboring classes and thereby increase the party's power base. Randolph's speeches made him famous, and his distinctive features, the joy of political cartoonists, made him a well-known figure in both Parliament and the pubs of the working classes.

To Winston, all this activity meant that his parents had less time for him than ever before. To make matters worse, he now had a baby brother to contend with as well. Now two little boys were shipped off for long visits with their grandparents at Blenheim or, infinitely preferable, for spring and summer holidays with Mrs. Everest's sister on the Isle of Wight.

There Winston felt truly carefree and cared for. Mrs. Everest's brother-in-law, a retired prison warden, had many wonderfully bloodcurdling stories about famous criminals and life in jails with which to captivate the young boy. Together, with the old man smoking his pipe, they would go for long tramps along the shore, and together they would sit and read the newspaper vigorously discussing the latest atrocities committed by the rebellious Zulu warriors against the gallant British troops. The two were fast friends.

Winston had no friend like that at home, and by the time he was seven his mother had started to describe her lonely elder son as a "troublesome boy." But a much worse peril than his mother's displeasure now menaced Winston. He was to go to school.

All his aunts and uncles assured him that school was a wonderful treat and that all his cousins were sorry to leave school to come home for their vacations. When his cousins refused to confirm these reports, Winston began to view the approaching adventure with more dread than anticipation. While eager for the companionship of other boys, and excited by the new wardrobe (including fourteen pairs of socks!) and equipment he was to take with him, he understood all too well that his playing days were over. From now on it would be seven or eight hours of lessons every day except Sunday and compulsory sports besides.

His misgivings were borne out on a bleak November day just before his eighth birthday. Dressed in stiff new clothes, he kissed Mrs. Everest good-bye and got into a waiting hansom cab with his mother. Winston's heart sank farther with every clop of the horse's hooves. The cab deposited them at the station, from which an all-too-swift train bore them to the town of Ascot and St. George's School. In the gloom of the afternoon Jennie and Winston took tea with the headmaster and his wife. Winston, small, frail, freckled, and red-headed, watched in amazement as the adults conversed easily. Weren't they worried about saying the wrong thing or spilling tea on the carpet? And how could his mother be so gay?

Suddenly Jennie got up, gave Winston a quick hug and three half-crowns for spending money, and left for home. For the first time in his life, Winston was alone with strangers. The headmaster immediately marched the boy down the corridor to a classrom, where a stern-faced teacher set him to work learning the first declension of Latin nouns. Fortunately, Winston's wonderful memory helped him accomplish the task easily, although it made no sense to him. But when he asked why there should be a special form of the word "table" to be used only when speaking to it (something, Winston pointed out, he never did), he was told that his impertinence would be severely punished.

Winston soon learned what that meant. Once a week recalcitrant students were summoned to the headmaster's office, divested of their trousers, and whipped until they bled while their classmates listened to their screams from the room next door. Although St. George's boasted small classes, a swimming pool and playing fields, a private chapel, and the wonders of electric light, in regard to discipline, it was medieval.

Winston spent two years there in a constant state of anxiety. He made little progress in schoolwork, always ranking at the bottom of his class. He was even more hopeless at sports. Frustration and fear led to bad behavior. One teacher referred to him as a "regular pickle" who once kicked in the headmaster's good straw hat after being flogged. His reports for the next year were no better. "He has no ambition," remarked one perceptive tutor. Another added that he was a "constant trouble to everybody and is always in some scrape or other." The boy just refused to cooperate academically or socially.

Perhaps it was Mrs. Everest's noticing the welts on Winston's backside that did it, for in 1884 his parents removed him from the school and dispatched him to an establishment in Brighton run by the Misses Thomson. The atmosphere here was kinder; his bottom would be safe from further assaults. Better still, the curriculum included things that interested Winston: French, history, poetry, riding, and swimming. His conduct was still horrible, but his scholarship improved to the point where his teachers could glimpse the makings of a fine student. He applied himself to Greek and Latin, practiced conversing in French, enjoyed geometry, and polished his writing skills.

When he fell violently ill with pneumonia in 1886, his parents rushed to his bedside with the finest doctors they could find, but once Winston recovered he scarcely saw them again, despite repeated pleas for visits. Neither parent showed any great interest in their son. Upon hearing that Winston had been stabbed with a penknife by an angry classmate, Jennie immediately assumed it was Winston's fault. And Randolph, reading the news in a letter from his wife, could only comment: "What adventures Winston does have."

Mrs. Everest wrote with love, urging Winston to wear his coat and not sit around in wet boots. Jennie wrote only when Winston asked for money; it seemed to be the only kind of support she could give him. From Randolph he got even less. Ignoring the heartache behind the words "I should be very proud if you would write to me, Papa," the busy member of Parliament did not even stop for a brief visit with his son while campaigning in Brighton. Winston, who had been distributing Randolph's autograph by the dozens to clamoring classmates, was crushed at not being able to show off his famous father.

Randolph was then at the height of his career. Thirty-seven years old, his influence in the Conservative Party was

so great that, after the Liberal defeat in 1886, he became leader of the House of Commons and chancellor of the Exchequer (a cabinet post similar to the American secretary òf the treasury). He held that job for less than six months. In December of that year, as he prepared and presented a budget calling for great reductions in military spending, Randolph was so sure of his power that he declared himself totally committed to defending his plan. When the prime minister told him that the proposed cuts were impossible, Randolph resigned, gambling that he was more important to the government than was the budget. He was wrong. His resignation was accepted on the spot. Randolph, having thrown away his chance for leadership in one reckless gesture, never held office again. Although he remained in Parliament, he found nothing but disappointment and failure in the rest of his public life.

There was more to Randolph's resignation than bravado, however. He was by now dying by inches of an illness that would eventually destroy his body and mind: syphilis. He looked far older than his years; his speech was sometimes slurred and his movements awkward; and there were times when his behavior could only be described as bizarre. Disease, just as much as pride, destroyed Randolph.

Winston knew nothing of his father's sickness and even little beyond the newspaper accounts of his resignation. He understood that a great political disaster had occurred, but because of the unwritten code ordering that such things were not discussed in front of strangers, servants, or children, he couldn't realize the extent of the crisis. He had other things on his mind anyway. Almost twelve years old, Winston would soon outgrow the pleasant school at Brighton and

*Winston at age twelve,*
*the year before he entered*
*Harrow, with his mother,*
*Lady Jennie Churchill*

have to go on to public school (the English equivalent of an American private preparatory school.)

But such a move was not as simple as packing your books and clothes and presenting yourself to the establishment of your choice. First you had to prove yourself worthy of admission by passing a series of tests. For Winston

> these examinations were a great trial. . . . the questions which they asked . . . were almost invariably those to which I was unable to suggest a satisfactory answer. . . . When I would willingly have displayed my knowledge, they sought to expose my ignorance. This sort of treatment had only one result: I did not do well in examinations.

Certainly his first experience in the "unhospitable regions of examinations" bears out this assertion. Winston's parents decided to send him to Harrow, because its location on a hill would be best for the boy's delicate lungs. On a breezy March day in 1887 Winston and one of his teachers journeyed from Brighton to take Harrow's entrance exam. Although he had been preparing for months, Winston was so anxious that he was sick to his stomach. He felt worse when the proctor handed him the questions and a blank sheet of paper. Winston's mind went blank too. He managed to write his name at the top of the paper, then boldly drew the number 1. Further consideration led him to enclose the number in brackets. A few inkblots of mysterious origin were the only other marks on the sheet Winston turned in two hours later.

All the way back to Brighton Winston insisted that he'd done so poorly because he'd never translated any Latin before. His Latin teacher, recognizing his nervous despair, decided not to contradict him. But miracles do sometimes happen, perhaps more often to sons of prominent men, and the next day Winston heard that he'd been accepted at Harrow.

Miracles only accomplish so much, however. Winston's performance placed him in the lowest division of the lowest grade. His hyphenated last name, Spencer-Churchill, reinforced his humble position by keeping him at the end of the alphabetical lists and lines. Unable to bear the jokes about Randolph Churchill's son being the very last of all, Winston dropped the Spencer from his name forever.

His lowly status did have one great advantage for him. Harrow's curriculum, while offering natural science, mathematics, and modern languages, still aimed at making every Harrovian as familiar with the ancient world as with his own. But the boys at the bottom of the school were exempted from most of the Greek and Latin. Considered "such dunces that we could learn only English," Winston and a few classmates came into the care of one man whose solemn duty it was to teach the stupidest boys "the most disregarded thing— namely to write mere English." As it took Winston three years to pass out of the lowest grade, he got the basics of English structure and composition into his bones. He always felt this was far more useful than being able to translate Caesar.

The character traits that Winston had cultivated at his preparatory schools blossomed at Harrow. He was frequently in trouble with authority or peers, and his scholastic progress was the despair of the masters. Yet Winston could apply himself when he wanted to. Thanks to hard work and a good memory, he won a prize for reciting twelve hundred lines of poetry without a single mistake. The staff recognized the contradiction. The first report sent to the Churchills complained that his "slovenliness," his constant lateness and infinite capacity for losing books and papers had gotten worse as the term wore on, and urged the Churchills to speak "very gravely" to their son. "As far as his ability goes he might be at the top of his form," the master continued, "whereas he is at the bottom." Without rapid reform, there would be no success for Winston at public school.

Winston's conduct may have been another play for his parents' attention. He still wrote regularly asking for more money than a thirteen-year-old could possibly need, but the odd shilling tucked into the return envelopes no longer appeased him. By misbehaving and getting poor grades,

Winston may have been telling his parents that since they obviously didn't care about *him,* he saw no reason why he should care about school, which obviously mattered to *them.*

Was Winston's perception wrong? His father was too busy to care about his foolish son; his mother, celebrating the many pleasures of life, didn't wish to be bothered with his troubles. Even by the standards of the day (and Victorian parents believed in rigorous schooling for, and physical separation from, their children), the Churchills' neglect of their older son was unusual. Oddly, the younger boy suffered no lack of attention. Only Winston's pathetic pleas for visits went unanswered.

Except by Mrs. Everest. She faithfully wrote to her former charge and came to see him as often as she could. On these occasions Winston would show her around as a guest of honor, openly hugging and kissing her. One time this affectionate behavior proved too much for his schoolmates. They thought it ridiculous that a boy of his age should kiss his old nurse in public and agreed to punish the culprit. That night they threw Winston on his bed and rolled him up in his mattress, nearly suffocating him. Then they poured hot and cold water over him. The providential appearance of a teacher put an end to the torture, and the spluttering, red-faced Winston was allowed to get up. He immediately began to berate his tormentors, ending his diatribe with a defiant "One day I shall be a great man and you shall be nobodies, and then I will stamp and crush you!"

Randolph accepted the school reports at face value and reconciled himself to the fact that his son was not university material; he had the boy switched into the army class instead. For many years, Winston thought that this new direction had been prompted by his flair in planning campaigns for toy soldiers, not a lack of respect for his intellect.

From then on the focus of Winston's studies was military. The army class was a world within Harrow, bent on nothing more than sending its members into England's military colleges and thence into the world as officers in Her Majesty's forces. To Winston's dismay, this brave new world still encompassed Latin, and Latin was something he could not master. Private tutoring was no use; in fact, Winston often noticed a look of physical pain on the tutor's face when he read his translations. For a while Winston swapped English essays for Latin compositions, but that scheme had to be abandoned when the English teacher detected Winston's style in two sets of papers.

And his style was already distinctive. Love of the language and the practice of rhetoric made him an accomplished writer early in his school career, although at times he did get carried away with lofty phrases and rolling rhythms. At Harrow he used his literary gifts to publish anonymous criticisms in the school paper, as well as to pay for his Latin homework.

Writing was a talent he also needed for preparing the history papers that were so important to an officer's training, and Winston had a lot of training ahead of him. Once he left Harrow at the age of eighteen, he would continue his education as a cadet at the Royal Military College at Sandhurst— that is, if he could pass the entrance examination. He had no trouble with the preliminary round, but he failed the next set. His old bugaboo of mathematics, that "hopeless bog of nonsense," had always mired him down, and now it kept him from collecting the proper number of points for admission.

Fresh from this failure, Winston went home for a brief holiday late in 1892 to find his parents almost at their wits' ends about him. To distract himself, Winston took his rifle and went hunting. Just outside the door, under his father's window, he saw a rabbit, and without thinking took aim and fired. The rabbit bolted for the woods, leaving Winston alone to face his father's angry curses. Suddenly noticing the distress in his son's face, Randolph changed his tone, and

proceeded to talk to me in the most wonderful and captivating manner about school and going into the army and the grown-up life which lay beyond. I listened spellbound to this sudden complete departure from his usual reserve, amazed at this intimate comprehension of all my affairs. Then at the end he said, "Do remember that things do not always go right with me. My every action is misjudged and every word distorted. . . . So make some allowances.

It was one of the three or four intimate talks Winston ever had with his father, and as he recalled, the only time he "lifted his visor in my sight."

Winston shattered any hopes for a fonder relationship with his father when he failed the Sandhurst exam the second time. By now the Churchills were hoping that one of their friends in the financial world might find a clerking job for him, since he was too much of a dunce even to get into the army. But they still had one more card to play. They'd heard of a professional crammer named Captain James. It was reported that anyone who was not a born idiot could not avoid getting into Sandhurst with his help, because he knew "with papal infallibility" which questions would be on the exam. They'd try him first.

But Winston nearly missed the chance to study with James. In January 1893, while visiting his aunt, he joined his cousins in a wild game of hide-and-seek. After twenty minutes of chase, Winston found himself trapped on a bridge across a pine-filled ravine. Rather than be captured, he decided to jump, figuring that the trees would break his thirty-foot fall to ground. As he later wrote, "the argument was correct, the data were absolutely wrong." The younger boys ran back to the house shouting "Winnie jumped from the bridge and won't speak to us!" He didn't regain consciousness for three days and didn't leave his bed until his ruptured kidney had had sufficient time to heal.

He recuperated at his parents' house in London. As his health improved, he was allowed to join them for meals, and sometimes he could accompany his father to parliamentary debates. From his seat in the Visitors' Gallery Winston observed the etiquette of the House of Commons, the proper forms of address and argument that made the business of the realm run as smoothly as possible. The young man also marveled at how the members could say such cruel and insulting things to each other in the House and then clap each other on the back and go out for a friendly dinner. But what he liked best of all was the chance to be with his father and to be recognized as "Randolph's boy."

In March a shaky Winston began working with Captain James. Progress was slow at first, and the captain, fearing that he'd met the student who would wreck his reputation, urged Randolph to speak to the boy about his "casual manner." Winston, it seemed, tended to be either inattentive or inclined to teach his teachers, having decided that he knew all he needed of history. As for mathematics, Winston simply memorized the tables of cosines and tangents and prayed for the best.

What he got was second best. In June he passed the exam but was admitted to the cavalry because his overall score was too low for the infantry. Still, he was in, and six years of examinations were behind him. Reading his letter of acceptance, Winston rejoiced that this unhappy period, this time of unending worry, toil, and "purposeless monotony" was over. He had survived but could see no point in all his expensive schooling. "I would rather have been apprenticed as a bricklayer's mate," he wrote in his autobiography, "or run errands as a messenger boy, or helped my father dress the front windows of a grocer's shop. It would have been real; it would have been natural; it would have taught me more; and I should have done it much better. Also," he added, "I should have got to know my father, which would have been a joy to me."

Winston was always keenly aware that he had been deprived of his father's care and love. Although he admitted it was a "heavy loss," he maintained that being an emotional orphan forced him to develop "an independence and vigour of thought" that a father's guidance could not have given. Solitary trees grow strong, he said.

Curiously, Winston didn't resent his father's attitude. His Randolph was a great statesman, thoughtful, strong, purposeful, and popular with both great and poor. Winston adored him and never stopped trying to live up to what he thought were his expectations.

He eventually did become that brave imitation of his father, but the father he chose to imitate was a fantasy. Unable to comprehend the man he saw so infrequently, the man who had thrown away his career on a miscalculation, the man who, now deathly ill, shuffled into Parliament and slurred speeches full of incoherent ideas and grandiose plans, Winston simply invented the father he wanted and needed. This noble version guided his youth and helped him grow up in a home of unhappiness and neglect. This capacity to forge what he needed out of what was at hand was a talent that would help him all throughout his life.

# SOLDIER

# 2

"My dear Winston," wrote Randolph on August 9, 1893, "I am rather surprised at your tone of exultation over your inclusion in the Sandhurst list. There are two ways of winning an examination, one creditable, the other the reverse. You have unfortunately chosen the latter method, and appear to be much pleased with your success."

Winston read on with a sinking heart. This "harum scarum style of work," continued the letter, had never gotten him anywhere. The Sandhurst result proved that. Not only had Winston missed the infantry, but he had even failed to improve his marks from earlier tries. "This is the grand result that you come up among the second and third rate class who are only good for commissions in a cavalry regiment."

There it was then. His father thought he was second rate.

But Randolph had other arrows in his quiver. The cavalry was going to cost an extra £200 a year. If Winston's conduct and action at Sandhurst were similar to what they had been at other schools, then Randolph would feel no responsibility to support his son any further. Let him become a shabby, useless "social wastrel"; it would all be his own fault.

By return mail a chastened and saddened Winston assured his father that he would reform, adding, "I am very sorry indeed that I have done so badly." To prove his resolve, Winston accepted the infantry spot that became available when other applicants decided not to attend. He hated giving up the chance to ride, but how else could he show Randolph that he was starting "a new page in his life"?

On Friday, September 1, 1893, Cadet Churchill arrived at Sandhurst on the 12:20 train from London, a member of a group of 120 young men who hoped to become fully commissioned officers during the next sixteen months. Winston liked the place immediately, even though he lost no time writing to his father that the room he shared with two other cadets was divided to look like stalls in a stable. No curtains, carpets, or ornaments relieved its starkness; no hot water—and very little cold—comforted its occupants. "Of course it is very uncomfortable," wrote Winston, quickly adding, "altogether, I like the life."

It was certainly very different from life at Harrow. Reveille sounded at 6:30, and the cadets had to be in class by 7:00. They got no breakfast until 8:00 and after that had to fall in for a parade at 9:10. Classes filled the time from 10:20 to 1:50, followed mercifully by lunch at 2:00. Another parade from 3:00 to 3:45, gymnastics from 5:00 to 6:00, and dinner (which Winston soon learned to call "mess") at 8 finished the day. Latin was nowhere in the curriculum, but neither was English. The cadets only tackled the properly martial subjects of fortifications, tactics, topography, military law, and military administration.

Winston enjoyed the studies. It was, after all, rather like being back with his nursery battalions. But he found the physical exertion needed to get through each day totally exhausting. His 5-foot 6½-inch frame and 31-inch chest had been judged inadequate by his commanding officers, and he had to do extra exercises to build himself up to proper soldier size or risk losing his commission. The young man found himself working hard for the first time in his life, and soon realized that he was so much reformed that he was showing up ten minutes too early for everything.

Randolph noticed the changes in his son's habits and self-confidence. Instead of a "spend-what-you-get" allowance, he now granted Winston a quarterly budget to manage. And he began to invite Winston along to social and political gatherings where the young man could meet other members of the Conservative Party, and, for the first time, flirt with young women. After nineteen years of neglect, these occasions were paradise for Winston.

He finished his first set of Sandhurst exams in December 1893, ranking twentieth in his class and even getting a commendation for good conduct. His family was surprised and relieved. The success went right to his head, however, for soon Randolph was complaining that "Winston's standards declined as his self-confidence grew."

Part of this lapse was due to discontent. The longer he stayed at Sandhurst, the more Winston realized that physically and intellectually the infantry was the wrong place for him. Gingerly, he began lobbying for a spot in the Fourth Hussars, a cavalry regiment whose officers he knew socially. Randolph still wouldn't hear of it, so Winston worked on Jennie, writing her a long letter listing all the advantages of cavalry service. His career would flourish, he asserted, for promotions came quicker to horsemen, and besides, he could be stationed in India, with men under him, in no time at all. He also argued from economy, pointing out that the government, not parents, assumed the costs of the care of an officer's horses. Finally, he set out his "sentimental reasons," listing the splendid uniform, his love of horses, and the advantages of riding over walking.

Winston also began courting the Hussars' colonel and spending time with the regiment at their quarters in Aldershot. Randolph was meanwhile using his influence to get Winston into a crack infantry regiment, the Sixtieth Rifles. Before the two Churchills could confront each other over Winston's future, however, Randolph left England.

In June 1894 Randolph abruptly decided that a trip around the world was just what he needed. Lately he'd been feeling left out of things. Slipping ever more quickly into the "mental paralysis" that marks the last stage of syphilis, his increasingly bizarre behavior had all but ended his social life; at one dinner he squealed and pointed because the butler didn't serve him fast enough. And the same men who once sat spellbound in the House whenever Randolph spoke now slipped out the door whenever they saw him rise and stagger toward the podium.

His doctors were dismayed by his plans. And Jennie was devastated at the thought of giving up her social life. She hated leaving her lovers, friends, and even her sons for a year and dreaded as well introducing her husband to strangers abroad, but duty compelled her to go. They traveled with a doctor, and with a lead-lined casket.

Winston knew only that they'd be gone for twelve months. He used the time energetically, campaigning to get into the Hussars, running up debts, and borrowing money. Even his generous allowance didn't stop him from sending appeals for emergency funds around the globe. His canteen and mess bills were frequently overdue, but he regularly sent Mrs. Everest, who had been summarily dismissed after twenty years' service, a few pounds.

During his father's absence, Winston also embraced his first public cause. In the name of purity, the London County Council had forced the management of the Empire Theatre, a popular music hall, to stop selling drinks in the auditorium. This was more than a temperance move, for the bar was also a popular rendezvous for prostitutes. To protect the public from the twin evils of drink and sex, the Council insisted that screens be erected to separate the pure and impure entertainments. An outraged Winston wrote to the newspapers decrying the tyranny of prudes, pleading that the way to higher morality was through improved education and social conditions, not through censorship. When reasonable words failed, he and some Sandhurst friends joined the mob that tore down the screens one Saturday night. Mounting the debris, Winston addressed the rioters, urging them to back their physical acts with political ones and turn the guilty councilmen out of office. But in spite of all his efforts, the prudes won the battle, and the Empire closed.

Winston wrote his father about the campaign, hoping for approval, for Randolph himself had been a regular at the Empire. But Randolph was past caring. The doctors despaired of his life. Yet it wasn't until November 1894 that anyone told Winston of his condition; it simply wasn't something one discussed with children. The young man was shocked. He had never realized how ill Randolph was or even believed that there was anything seriously wrong. In his letters to Jennie there now appeared a new concern for her welfare, as well as his growing acceptance of his father's approaching death.

The Churchills returned to London on Christmas Eve, 1894. Exactly one month later Winston was wakened early and sent into the room where his father lay in a stupor. Randolph died painlessly and peacefuly. With him died all of Winston's hopes of friendship, of comradeship in Parliament, of love. Cheated of the chance to prove his true worth, Winston swore to pursue his father's aims and vindicate the man he believed Randolph was. Years later, when his own reputation was greater than his father's had ever been, Winston would often become withdrawn and mutter "Why could *he* not see what I have done?"

Twenty-year-old Winston was head of the family now. New status brought new problems. Randolph had left staggering debts, which meant that little money was available to his wife and sons. Jennie continued to spend and mortgage her private income at an alarming rate. Soon they would all be dependent on the young soldier who would shortly be serving in the Fourth Hussars with a total salary of £120 a year.

These financial worries, far from shackling Winston, actually freed him. Forced to rely on himself and his talents, Winston began to plan a life for himself. He would enter the cavalry as he wanted; he would make a fortune with sword and pen; he would ultimately enter Parliament and enjoy the political career he yearned for.

Within a month of Randolph's death, Winston joined the Hussars. He filled his rooms with rented furniture and took long hot baths to ease the aches of his daily two-hour riding class. The large Harrow contingent in the regiment welcomed their brother officer, and Winston contentedly contemplated his next four years of military life.

It would be wonderful to report that as a salaried officer earning his own keep Winston experienced a fiscal reformation. But such was not the case. He was in debt even before he formally took up his commission. Winston figured it cost him nearly £700 just to buy the horse he needed to join the Hussars. He also needed money for polo ponies so he could play on the regimental team. And the seven pairs of pants he ordered for himself along with the regulation uniforms and racing silks were not paid for until six years later.

Winston's conduct was less than ideal in other ways as well. Suddenly finding himself part of a clique after a lifetime without a close friend, he did whatever he had to do to keep his popularity and position, even if his actions went against his better nature. His friends tended to haze and torment other officers if they lacked at all in courage, riding skill, or money. Winston even rode in a rigged race. His crowd, in effect, was a gang of bullies.

Riding practice, drill, polo, and the easy companionship of the mess filled most of the time, and he was stationed close enough to London to occupy the other hours in seeing his mother and attending banquets and balls. He was also close enough to make a very important and sad journey in June 1895 to visit his beloved Woom, who lay dying.

*Winston cut a striking figure in the uniform of the Fourth Hussars.*

Winston arrived thoroughly soaked in the midst of a heavy rainstorm. From her bed Mrs. Everest insisted that he get out of his wet clothes at once lest he catch cold. Dashing back to camp for an early morning parade, Winston returned to her side as soon as possible. Neither her doctor nor the specialist Winston had called could help the old woman. All Winston could do was hold her hand until she slipped easily into unconsciousness. Having lost "the dearest and most intimate friend" he had ever known, Winston arranged her funeral and erected her monument. Within six months, he had lost the two people who had done the most to shape his character.

It is said that Alexander the Great wept when he realized that there were no more worlds for him to conquer. Winston and his brother officers did much the same. Britain had been frustratingly at peace for the past thirty years, and the odd skirmish or battle in some remote corner of the Empire offered no hope of action for a regiment comfortably settled in a London suburb. To the young subalterns in the summer of 1895, war, active service, medals, and glory all seemed to be going the way of the dinosaurs.

There was, however, one small blemish on the smiling face of peace. Spain had sent troops to the tiny island of Cuba to quash a native rebellion, one of several that had interrupted the profitable relationship enjoyed with its richest colonial possession. This current outbreak was the worst so far. Not only did rebel strength increase with the arrival of every troopship from the mother country, but the rest of the world was beginning to notice what was going on. While both popular and official opinion in the United States favored the rebel cause, Britain stood by its European ally.

To the dismay of the cavalry officers straining in their saddles, England's support was spiritual only. No troops or equipment would go to the New World, at least, not officially. Winston decided, however, that this remote war would be just the place to put his military temperament to the test, a private dress rehearsal for the time when he would actually defend Her Majesty under fire.

Winston convinced a friend that they should spend their five months' winter leave in Cuba. Their commanding officer gave them his blessing, pleased at the subalterns' initiative in finding something constructive to do with their time off. Permission from the Spanish Army was procured with the help of the British ambassador to Spain, who also happened to be an old family friend. Jennie, who had become much more supportive of her son since Randolph's death, kindly offered to pay for his passage as a birthday present. Winston also arranged to send letters from the front to the *Daily Graphic* for the sum of five guineas apiece, figuring that the extra money, and notoriety, could never hurt.

The two young soldiers were welcomed to New York, the first stop on their journey to the West Indies, on November 10, 1895, by one of Jennie's friends. He introduced them to New York society and arranged their sight-seeing, which included visits to West Point (where the two were horrified by the strict regulations) and to a murder trial. The three-day stopover stretched to a week before they continued south again.

On November 20 they sailed into Havana harbor, as full of excitement and anticipation as Long John Silver's crew upon reaching Treasure Island. They settled into Havana's finest hotel, "ate a great quantity of oranges, smoked a number of cigars," and then, full of these Cuban delights, presented their credentials to the Spanish authorities. Despite their protestations, the two were treated with the deference due an official embassy. And thanks to their influential connections everything was perfectly arranged for them.

The next day they boarded an armored train in order to catch up with a mobile column of soldiers and observe guerrilla warfare firsthand. Winston got his heart's desire for a twenty-first birthday present. When the army stopped for breakfast in a jungle clearing that day, he heard the whistle of enemy bullets for the first time. In fact, the horse tethered behind Winston, as he sat gnawing on a chicken drumstick, was hit and killed. Finally, he had been under fire.

Winston soon realized that the Cuban war could go on forever. The Spanish army marched around the island, and the Cuban rebels shot at them from the bush. No one ever met in set battle; the Spanish wouldn't even pursue their attackers fifty yards into the jungle. The Englishmen left the column when it had marched back to where they'd first met it, and sailed for England.

Winston was confused about his loyalties in this war. He sympathized with Cuban complaints about colonial abuses yet disapproved of their tactics. Nor did he think the Spanish army much better. Winston expressed these views in his dispatches to the *Daily Graphic.* His Spanish hosts complained of his ingratitude, but gave him a courtesy medal anyway.

The Cuban expedition proved to Winston that he could get along on his own. The *Graphic* articles showed him that journalism could win him fame and fortune, and consequently he returned to his regiment in an optimistic frame of mind.

The Hussars had moved to barracks closer to London, preparatory to leaving for a twelve-year posting in India. Drill and duties were curtailed so that the men would have enough time to put all their affairs in order. To Winston this was great fun. He lived at home with his mother, commuting to the barracks by underground railway two or three times a week. The rest of the time was his to read, play polo, and enjoy the delights of the social season.

As India drew nearer, Winston became more and more convinced that he didn't want to go. He needed action if he were to make the money and reputation that would get him into Parliament, and India was quiet those days. South Africa, where the Dutch Boers seemed to be getting restless, looked like a far better assignment for the ambitious subaltern. But none of his or Jennie's contacts could get him out of it, and Winston and twelve hundred others began their twenty-three-day voyage to Bombay in September 1896.

Winston spent the trip playing cards and chess but was nevertheless relieved when Bombay rose on the horizon.

Eager to be on terra firma once again, he and some friends hired a tiny boat to ferry them ashore before the others. Nearing the dock, the boat dipped away just as Winston reached out for a handhold. He felt a "peculiar wrench" and scrambled up, hugging his shoulder and cursing. His haste had caused him to dislocate his shoulder, and the injury was to plague him, and his polo playing, the rest of his life.

From Bombay, the Hussars traveled six hundred miles south to their station at Bangalore. There the officers lived like princes in private bungalows with staffs of servants to take care of man and horse. Winston devoted his leisure to collecting butterflies and growing roses. His army duties were usually finished by noon and rarely interfered with the lordly rhythms of the day, which inlcuded a long afternoon siesta followed by the "Hour of Polo," which lasted until dark. Winston was a devoted team member, always ready for another chukker or tournament, and spent most of his salary on his ponies.

But life in India soon palled. Starved for stimulation, Winston began reading during the siesta. Beginning with Gibbon's *Decline and Fall of the Roman Empire,* he worked his way through books on history, philosophy, religion, and, most significantly, he started reading the *Annual Register of Parliamentary Debates.* To sharpen his views and understand the workings of the House of Commons, he wrote his own opinions in the margins of these books before studying the arguments. Intent upon completing his education, Winston soon wrote to his mother asking for books as he had once asked for money.

Even intellectual exercise couldn't overcome his sense of boredom and isolation, however. He missed current newspapers, a social circle, and political gossip and saw no value in his Indian experience. He followed election results and thought of what he could be accomplishing in England; he read military reports and thought longingly of the active service that seemed to be forbidden to him. In short, he felt "out of the running" and worried that he would never be able to catch up with those his own age in England.

After eight months in India, Winston managed to get permission to take three months leave in England, something normally awarded only after serving three years in the East. Obsessed by the thought that he would be left behind, he reasoned that it would be worth using all his funds for the chance to make the contacts that Jennie, despite his entreaties, refused to make for him. He could call on his father's Conservative colleagues and visit some army people about his application for special service in Egypt with General Horatio H. Kitchener, who was reconquering the Sudan—or perhaps he would just stop off in Cairo on his way home to see if he could attach himself to anyone's staff. At this suggestion, Jennie was horrified and begged him not to jeopardize his position for the sake of a reputation that he hoped to make. "They will say, and with some reason that you can't stick to anything." Expressing her dismay at his career, she continued: "You seem to have no real purpose in life and won't realize at the age of 22 that for a man life means work, and hard work if you mean to succeed. Many men at your age have to work for a living and," she added, "support their mother." Winston chose not to hear Jennie's sermon, replying only that he hoped she wouldn't relax her efforts to get him to Egypt.

Once back in London, however, even Winston didn't pursue his military plans so strenuously. This was the year of Queen Victoria's Diamond Jubilee, and Winston didn't want to miss any of it.

Nor did he want to miss the chance to further his other goal—a career in politics. He presented himself at Conservative Party headquarters in July 1897, asking to address some meeting while on leave. Luck was with him again, for the party had been swamped with requests for speakers at rallies, meetings, and bazaars all over England. Winston chose a meeting at Bath to launch his oratorical career, and on July 26 delivered a speech on workmen's compensation that was well received by party members and the press.

Winston celebrated his debut with a day at the races. He was happily cashing in a winning ticket when he caught sight of a newspaper headline announcing the revolt of Pathan tribesmen on the northwest border of India and Afghanistan. Reading further, Winston realized that luck was indeed smiling on him that day. The general in charge of the British regiments being formed to tame the frontier had once promised Winston a place on his staff the next time he saw action. Telegraphing the general that he was on his way, Winston cut short his leave and took the next train for Brindisi and the steamer that would carry him back to India. At each port he expected to find his orders waiting. Not until he got to Bombay did he learn that he was too late—the staff was filled. He could, however, come on as an official correspondent and move to a staff position once a casualty occured. It looked as if Winston would soon command real troops in a real war.

In the meantime Winston tried to raise funds for his extra-curricular adventure by writing about it. Fortunately, both an Indian and an English paper wanted his columns. Getting reluctant permission for another leave from his commander, Winston packed his kit and began the five-day rail journey to the Khyber Pass where the Malakand Field Force was fighting.

Winston was thrilled to be in the midst of battle and reveled in being able to hold his ground when everyone else was taking cover. No act was too daring for him as long as it had witnesses and might lead to a medal. Winston was quite frank about his glory hunting. He needed a reputation to break into politics. Besides, he comforted Jennie in a letter from the front, "bullets . . . are not worth considering. . . . I am so conceited I do not believe the Gods would create so potent a being as myself for so prosaic an ending."

Winston's conceit was crushed when he learned that Jennie had had his fifteen dispatches to England published anonymously. He wanted publicity and acclaim. He also wanted to show the truth of his new belief: that he was put on earth for some special purpose. "I have faith in my star, that is that I am intended to do something in the world." This idea seemed to have come out of nowhere, but its power was strong. Winston was trying to prove it with his life.

In October he was ordered back to the Fourth Hussars. His way of picking and choosing his war service was beginning to annoy his fellow officers on the frontier, and for the sake of peace in the camp, Winston was sent back to Bangalore. There he consoled himself by turning his articles into a book, working at great speed to beat another war correspondent into print. Although *The Story of the Malakand Field Force* dripped gore and suffered from poor editing, this candid criticism of British policy sold well, and Winston basked in the praise he got from the press, members of the government, and even the prince of Wales.

While with his regiment, Winston also wrote a semiautobiographical novel called *Savrola*. A romantic tale of love, intrigue, and war, it was praised for its war notes and panned for its style and characters. With its publication, Winston abandoned the field of fiction.

In the summer of 1898 he again returned to England on leave. He spoke at more Conservative meetings, and his success on the podium strengthened his determination to pursue a life of politics. But he still needed money and fame to launch his career.

He and Jennie redoubled their efforts to get him into Kitchener's Egyptian force. Kitchener, however, who knew about Winston's free-lance warring and writing as well as his intention to leave the army, refused to take him on. It took a letter from the prime minister and a fortuitous vacancy in the Twenty-first Lancers to send Winston up the Nile. Once again, notebook and pencil were in his kit bag, for he was selling articles once more. This time the money was more grimly essential. In order to go to Egypt, Winston had to agree to absolve the British government of any financial responsibility for his welfare. If he were wounded, he would get no aid or compensation.

Winston found himself at war within the camp as well as beyond its perimeter. His shameless glory seeking antagonized his brother officers, and he and Kitchener eyed each other with mutual contempt. Out in the desert, the Egyptians were fierce opponents. Winston met them at Omdurman, joining the British army's last great cavalry charge—two minutes of slashing, shooting, and screaming that left 48 dead and 428 wounded. While Winston survived untouched, he was sent home with his sadly depleted regiment.

Winston was glad to have been part of the charge and to have served with Kitchener, but he was even gladder to have a fresh set of dispatches to turn into another best seller, *The River War*. Reviewers praised its prose but censured the author for his negative portrait of Kitchener and indelicate criticism of the conduct of the campaign. Thanks to Winston's literary efforts, the post of officer-correspondent disappeared from the ranks of the British army. No one else would ever fight and write for pay.

But authorship and the routine of army life could no longer allay Winston's political hopes, and in March 1899, believing his writing would pay his way, Winston resigned his commission. He stayed in India just long enough to help the Hussars win their first Inter-Regimental Polo Tournament (despite playing with a dislocated shoulder and sprained ankles) and then sailed for home, leaving the adventures of the military battlefield for, he hoped, the battlefield of Parliament. He knew it was the right time. The army was too confining for his ambitions. He was meant for greater things.

# PRISONER

# 3

In England, Winston presented himself to Conservative Party leaders as a candidate for a seat in the House of Commons. It was the logical move for him to make, and the party expected to see him. Winston was already known for his egocentric and self-expressive manner, and his courage and ambition were admired, albeit grudgingly, by his peers. They might not like his ungentlemanly pursuit of power, but all who met him were impressed with his sense of his own strength, destiny, and greatness.

Winston had more behind him than self-confidence, of course. He intended to use his father's reputation and connections to their fullest advantage. And his well-developed views on politics and international affairs, formed during those long Indian afternoons, helped make him a knowledgeable and sophisticated candidate as well.

He'd already decided to follow the political path of his father. Advocating universal male suffrage, universal education, local self-government, eight-hour workdays, and a progressive income tax, Winston also favored salaries for members of Parliament. A strong navy, an imperial defense system, whereby Britain's colonies would contribute to defense, and nonintervention in European disputes were the main supports of his opinions on foreign affairs.

Eager to have the magical Churchill name to trade on once again, the Conservatives found Winston a constituency in Oldham, a textile town in Lancashire. (Members of Parliament do not have to live in the districts they represent.) Winston threw himself enthusiastically into his campaign, speaking at several meetings a day, attending rallies, and even getting his family to do some handshaking and babykissing. He seemed to be immensely popular with the voters, but they chose his opponent anyway. Winston lost graciously. As one reporter noted: "A smile lighted up his features, and the result of the election did not disturb him. He might have been defeated, but he was conscious that in this fight he had not been disgraced." He was also aware that this race was only a minor setback. He'd done well enough to reckon that it would only be a matter of months before he'd enter the House of Commons.

But Winston could not wait idly. He found another war to join.

In 1899 the British in Cape Colony at the southernmost tip of Africa had started fighting with the Dutch Boers (farmers) in the Transvaal Republic to the north. Although Britain had annexed the Transvaal more than twenty years earlier, the Dutch had recently reasserted their independence, arming themselves and denying rights to the British *uitlanders* who thought they could settle anywhere in South Africa. When British troops arrived at the Transvaal border to ensure that right, war was inevitable.

Her Majesty's troops expected to be back at their barracks within three months. They didn't know about the Boer arms shipments from Germany and Holland, the cannon, rifles, and ammunition hidden all over the countryside. Nor had they reckoned on Boer tactics. Expert riflemen and riders, the Dutch refused to meet the British in set battle, preferring to appear suddenly out of the bush to immobilize the enemy in a surprise raid. These commandos kept the British at a perpetual disadvantage, and the war settled in for a long and fitful spell.

To Winston, the Boer War seemed made to order. He quickly convinced the *Morning Post* to send him to South Africa as their correspondent for a handsome wage: £1,000 for the first four months of his stay and £200 a month thereafter, plus all expenses and the copyright to his articles. Then he packed his bags and boarded a steamer.

Once in Capetown, Winston arranged an army commission for himself and then, with two sets of credentials tucked into his jacket pocket, continued by ship through the stormy East African seas to Durban and the fighting.

The day after meeting the British troops Winston began the adventure that would bring him the fame and triumph he so longed for. He was traveling by armored train on a reconnaissance mission into enemy territory when a well-placed stone derailed several cars. The British soldiers suddenly found themselves trying to do two things at once: free the engine from the wreckage and defend themselves from the Boer bullets that whizzed by as soon as the first Englishman jumped from the train. Winston directed the line-clearing operations and after several hours crammed himself into the engine with the wounded soldiers for the trip back to Durban.

Suddenly realizing that the commanding officer and several others were still at the site of the wreck, Winston jumped down and walked back along the track to offer his help. Just as he remembered that his pistol was still on board, he saw his comrades raise a white flag. The train was now almost out of sight. There was nothing to do but walk on and be taken prisoner with the others.

The journey to the converted officers' school in Pretoria that was serving as a prison was a gloomy one for all but Winston. As the commanding officer recalled, the soldiers were "disconsolate . . . but Churchill must have been

cheered by the thought, which he communicated to me, that what had taken place, though it had caused the loss of his post as a correspondent, would help considerably in opening the door for him to enter the House of Commons.'' Beneficial as his capture might be to his career, Winston certainly had no intention of staying in prison. On arrival in Pretoria, he began petitioning for his release, claiming the neutrality of a war correspondent. The Boers, however, knew that Winston's efforts had helped the train to get away and turned down every request.

Winston saw no alternative but to escape, and convinced two other officers to let him in on their plans. The trio made several false attempts, but one night all conditions were perfect. As two guards stood talking quietly together, Winston and his cohorts strolled over to the lavatory shed nearest the fence. In a minute Winston had climbed up and out through the window and quickly scrambled over the fence. He was free at last. Crouching in the bushes, he waited for his companions. They never came. Many hours later one of them reentered the lavatory and whispered through the window that the guards were suspicious, it was too dangerous, and could Winston get back in?

Winston stood up. He would have to go on alone now. In his pockets were a bar of chocolate and £75. No map, no compass could guide him out of Dutch territory. He couldn't even ask directions without giving himself away, for he knew no Dutch. But he had no choice—he couldn't go back to jail. Pulling his cap well down over his face, Winston strode through the streets of Pretoria, forcing himself to walk slowly and not look back, humming softly under his breath. Eventually, as the houses became fewer, he came to a railway line.

*Winston went to South Africa as a correspondent for the* Morning Post.

He knew he needed to board a train to escape Pretoria, but which way led to free Portuguese territory in the east and which deeper into Boer land?

Winston jumped onto the next train that passed, anxiously searching the sky for the first signs of daybreak. Once he realized that he was indeed heading east, he breathed a little easier, but still left the train before it was fully light enough for him to be seen. He had no idea where he was but understood that he had to wait until dusk to follow the tracks again. Throughout that long day, he remembered, "my sole companion was a gigantic vulture, who manifested an extravagant interest in my condition, and made hideous and ominous gurglings from time to time."

News of Winston's escape spread quickly among the prisoners. None of them was especially pleased. The two men who had devised the plan were galled at being left behind; others complained that Winston, who wasn't even a proper officer, had ruined their own chances of escape. Resentment didn't keep them from covering Winston's tracks, however. Someone rolled a blanket and tucked it into Winston's bed. Early next morning the guard offered it a cup of tea. But the barber who came to shave him at 8 found the dummy and raised the alarm. Searching the room for clues, prison officials found only Winston's handwritten letter of explanation and regret at not being able to make personal farewells to the authorities.

Alone in the country, Winston now thought only about survival. As dusk approached and no trains passed, he decided to make his way to a small house near what looked like a mine entrance. Knocking boldly, he told the man who answered that he'd had an accident and needed food badly. The man silently beckoned him in, sat down at a table, and, making sure that Winston saw the gun in his lap, asked for the real story.

Winston confessed everything. But Destiny had spared him once again. Winston had stumbled into the home of the only English sympathizer for miles around.

The man hid Winston in an unused portion of the mine, smuggling food from his table in a napkin so his Dutch servants wouldn't notice. For everyone knew of Winston's escape. Posters everywhere offered a £25 reward, dead or alive, for a man

> 25 years old, about 5 ft 8 in tall, walks with a slight stoop, pale appearance, red brown hair, almost invisible small moustache, speaks through his nose, cannot pronounce the letter "s", cannot speak Dutch, has last been seen in a brown suit of clothes.

After three days in the mine, sleeping on top of food and candles to protect them from the free-roaming rats, Winston was given a sack of food and a pistol and huddled aboard an eastbound freight. He scrambled under a tarpaulin and tried to relax. He knew he had a three-day journey ahead of him, yet he was afraid to move, afraid even to sleep, lest he snore and be discovered. On the third day he peeked out as the train passed a station and thought he recognized Portuguese uniforms on the guards. When he saw them again at the next station he knew he was out of Dutch territory. "Then," he wrote in his autobiography, "as we rambled and banged along, I pushed my head out of the tarpaulin and sang and shouted and crowed at the top of my voice." He also fired two shots in the air from the sheer joy of being free.

Winston climbed stiffly off the train at the capital of Portuguese East Africa and made his way to the British Consulate. There he enjoyed a hot bath, a good dinner, and unlimited use of the telegraph to tell the world he was alive before returning to British territory. A cheering crowd waving Union Jacks greeted him at the dock at Durban. His escape had made him a hero.

The hero chose to stay on in South Africa. He still wrote to the English press about the extent of Boer strength, and to prove his commitment to the British cause, he joined the native South African Light Horse Regiment. Wearing a fine plumed hat, he helped fight the final battles of the war.

His last few months in Africa were brightened by the presence of his family. His brother was serving there, and Jennie, who had "raised a fund, captivated an American millionaire, obtained a ship and equipped it as a hospital," was there too. Winston found the life pleasant: "We lived in great comfort in the open air, with cool nights and bright sunshine, with plenty of meat, chicken, and beer."

But all good things come to an end, and in July 1900, when it was obvious that Boer resistance had been broken, Winston returned to England. He'd had quite a year. He'd made a name for himself at home and abroad; he'd made friends, and enemies, in high places; he'd won his reputation for courage; he'd confirmed that he could support himself by writing. At age twenty-five Winston felt good and ready to make his mark.

The next year was just as exciting. Shortly after coming home, Winston watched his mother marry George Cornwallis West, a man just his age. And while waiting for the next election, he polished off two books on the Boers. Both enjoyed good reviews and brisk sales. Combined with his newspaper stories, Winston had earned £4,000 from the war.

In late autumn he finally won the seat for Oldham. With a few months to spare before the opening of Parliament Winston embarked on a lecture tour. Packing his South African notes and magic-lantern slides, he thrilled audiences in church halls and assembly rooms all over England with his adventures. After giving twenty-nine talks in thirty days, he took his show to America. Strong pro-Boer sentiment in the States made this venture less triumphant and profitable, but he did address a full house at New York's Carnegie Hall. That night he was introduced by Mark Twain, who explained to the audience that "Mr. Churchill by his father is an Englishman, by his mother an American, no doubt a blend that makes the perfect man."

Although he complained about speaking an hour or more, and sometimes twice, every day but Sunday, and about never sleeping in the same bed two nights running, Winston felt proud. "There is not one person in a million who at my age could have earned £10,000 without any capital in two years," he boasted.

The future beckoned brightly.

# POLITICIAN

# 4

Sitting on the members' benches in Commons for the first time in February 1901, Winston resolved to devote himself exclusively to his political career. His attendance was exemplary. Despite the odd days off for lecturing, hunting, and playing polo, he rarely missed a debate and even delivered nine major speeches that first year. His maiden speech dealt with British policies in South Africa, but he ended his remarks with a short tribute to his father. The press loved it. Within three months Winston was confident enough to urge both army reform and magnanimity toward the defeated Boers. He was also warning the House of the "ruin and exhaustion" any future European war would bring.

Somehow that year he also found time to add to his prestige and his purse by writing a biography of his father. While it enshrined the idealized political genius Winston believed Lord Randolph to have been, later historians have discounted the work as a "systematic whitewashing."

Winston spent most of his spare time with a group of other young Conservative M.P.'s with liberal inclinations. With them, Winston hoped to restore the tattered flag of Randolph's Tory Democracy, or at least his interpretation of it. Such filial devotion at first amused the party leaders, then annoyed them. Young Winston was operating on the assumption that a member's only loyalty was to himself, that all he had to do was decide what was right and state it clearly. He obviously did not understand the strict needs or subtle nuances of party loyalty.

By 1903 this assumption had him in trouble with the party. Winston believed free trade was best for England and his constituency; his party preferred protective tariffs. When Winston rose to speak against the levies, his Conservative colleagues left the House en masse. Unwilling to sacrifice his principles to keep his Conservative friends and a secure seat, Winston entered the House on a day in May, bowed to the presiding Speaker, crossed the floor, and took a seat in the Liberal benches.

Some saw Winston's defection to the Liberal Party as class as well as political treason. Certain social invitations stopped, fellow M.P.'s cut him in the corridors, and he was even blackballed by his polo club. The newborn Liberal made matters worse by attacking his old party in his speeches; now he was not only hated by Conservatives but also distrusted by the Liberals. And his tendency to draw his personal friends from both sides of the political fence made everyone nervous, for it was a sure sign that he didn't take the party system seriously.

He might have had to work hard to prove himself, but he could scarcely have chosen a better time to switch affiliations. The Conservative Party was in decline, and for the next seventeen years Liberals would captain the British ship of state. Winston was determined to join them on the bridge.

The Liberal government elected in 1905 saw the advantages of keeping Winston a contented party member and was quick to offer him a junior cabinet post. With uncommon confidence, Winston refused the treasury job they first suggested. He held out for the post of undersecretary for the colonies, an office he described as "not one of any great responsibility" but of "possibilities—both towards danger and success." Winston saw the empire threatened by colonial demands for independence and wanted to preserve Britain's power. This job was the place from which to stage his fight. He would be the one to lead debates in Commons, to propose and defend colonial policy, to decide questions of home rule, and, more to the point, to direct the South African settlement.

Winston's tenure in the Colonial Office was not an easy time for anyone, politically or personally. The new undersecretary had many clashes with his boss, and his fellow officials disliked the way he high-handedly rewrote the speeches and replies they drafted for his use in Parliament. This most junior minister also disturbed the cabinet consensus by fervently defending his own opinions against his seniors' collective judgment. But he was making a name for himself. By the time he was thirty-two Winston had already seen a biography of himself in print. Buoyed by his growing reputation, proud of his accomplishments, Winston was able to lean across the dinner table one night and confide to his partner, "We are all worms. But I do believe that I am a glowworm."

Even glowworms get tired, however. In 1907 he arranged a trip to East Africa for himself. Officially, he was going to determine the best way to handle the development of British territory there; unofficially, he was going hunting. True to form, he found a magazine to underwrite his personal expenses. At every stop Winston sent two dispatches: one to the office and one to the magazine.

The trip soon took on the trappings of a royal tour. British officials greeted him and arranged banquets and festivities in his honor. At one place, Winston asked to borrow some camels so he could do some private sight-seeing. The man in charge, annoyed by the request, sent the stableboy off with the worst-tempered beast in the lot for Winston. The boy returned that evening with a wide grin and a generous tip. When asked what had happened, the boy said: "Sahib camel kick Churchill. Churchill sahib kick camel. Him very good camel now, sahib."

The tour ended with a safari through the African interior.

Three hundred fifty porters carried the baggage and supplies. It was the high spot of Winston's trip. He was able to shoot a white rhinocerous and infuriate his companions by retiring each night with a cheerful "Sofari, sogoody."

Once back in London, Winston rushed *My African Journey* into print. He also began turning his mind from colonial disputes to social welfare. "Minimum standards of wages and comfort," he wrote in 1908, "insurance in some effective form against sickness, unemployment, old age—these are the questions . . . by which parties are going to live in the future." Winston also started actively supporting a working-class franchise and compulsory education.

His advocacy was well timed. In 1908 he was named president of the Board of Trade; in this capacity he would oversee matters of labor and commerce. Winston, once again in the right place at the right time, accepted on condition that the job be raised to full cabinet rank. Determined to wage war against poverty, he believed that the government should guide the economy by taking up where private industry left off and that a new cabinet office was the best place to direct operations or, as he put it, "a good place to interfere from."

At the age of thirty-three, Winston was the youngest cabinet member to serve in nearly half a century. Now, instead of dealing with the Boer government, he filled his days with questions about lighthouse keepers' wages, improved lighting in railway stations, and daylight savings time. He also shaped his sprawling department into a well-tuned instrument for social reform. Within two months of taking office, Winston was badgering cabinet officers twenty years his senior to cut military spending not only because it was one of his father's causes but because he felt that the money spent on guns could be better applied to social programs.

And he had several in mind. Struck by the then novel idea that laborers should be able to see their families during daylight hours, he proposed legislation limiting working hours. Along with the radical Liberal David Lloyd George, he devised ways to abolish sweatshops, to guarantee minimum wages and a tea break, to provide the unemployed with insurance, and to create labor exchanges where they could find work. Winston's energy and ability were astounding. Although some cabinet ministers feared that he would soon turn his eyes on their departments, others marked him as a future prime minister. He had the tenacity, courage, drive, and ambition needed for the job or, in other words, the proper balance of "genius and plod."

From the mountaintop he had reached, Winston could survey the landscape with satisfaction. He'd certainly proved his father wrong about his capabilities. With a powerful position and a more than adequate income already his, he could see only one more world to conquer. It was time to marry.

In March 1908, shortly before moving to the Board of Trade, Winston found himself seated at a dinner party next to Clementine Hozier. One of the most beautiful women in England, Clementine was also a heartbreaker who had broken off two engagements. Fascinated, Winston talked to her all evening, even forgoing the masculine privilege of port and cigars. His conversation, not surprisingly, was mainly about himself.

For the next few months he pursued her as single-mindedly as anything else he had done. They wrote often, but rarely met. In August he invited her to Blenheim for the weekend, and there, in an ornamental temple where they were waiting out a sudden shower, he proposed. That night Clementine sent him a simple note: "Winston," with a heart drawn around it.

They were married before eight hundred guests in London on September 12, 1908. Winston, for once pale, appeared in a suit the popular press called "one of the greatest failures as a wedding garment" ever seen. Clementine's composure was marred by last-minute doubts. But although their vows were barely audible beyond the front pews, once the ceremony was over the two regained their confidence, walking down the aisle as if getting married were an everyday event. Winston even stopped to talk politics with Lloyd George in the vestry.

Winston often said that persuading Clementine to marry him was his greatest achievement; in fact, he ended his autobiography with the words "I married and lived happily ever after." Marriage was not so simple for the new Mrs. Churchill, however. Sensing her future as she watched her husband pack official papers in their honeymoon baggage, she knew it for sure when he passed up a gondola ride in the Venetian moonlight for a trip in a "quicker and more hygienic" boat.

Their union endured for nearly sixty years. Both having experienced unhappy childhoods, they were able to provide comfort, security, and a home for each other. Together they built their own world of pet names, baby talk, and the thousand personal traditions that give shape and strength to a marriage. Within a year they were parents. Diana, born in July 1909, was, her father boasted, "the prettiest child ever seen. . . . She is exactly like me."

But even the newfound delights of family life could not distract Winston from politics. With other Liberals, he helped to draft what came to be known as the "People's Budget," which sought to raise money for massive social legislation by taxing the rich more than ever. The Conservative House of Lords, the upper chamber of Parliament, whose membership was hereditary rather than elective, threatened to veto the budget, effectively killing all hopes of reform. Winston saw the budget as a constitutional issue. Here was the perfect vehicle to break the power of the House of Lords and bring England into the twentieth century. In a pamphlet called *The People's Rights,* he argued that social change could be enacted only by denying the veto power of the Lords. Once again he was denounced as a class traitor.

When the Lords rejected the People's Budget in 1910, the prime minister dissolved the government and called a general election. Although a Liberal majority was returned, the cabinet was reshuffled. Afraid that Winston would dismantle the armed forces if put in charge of them as he requested, the prime minister appointed him instead to the office of Home Secretary.

Promotion to a major cabinet office meant many changes for Winston. For one thing, it doubled his salary, making it somewhat easier to support his family, house, and four servants. It also meant that he would leave the path of direct social reform for the numerous byways of the Home Office. While he could still lobby for welfare legislation, he would now spend his days solving questions of immigration, censorship, and hunting and his nights writing a report to the king on the day's parliamentary activity.

One of the first problems the new home secretary turned his energies to was prison reform. A government report had recently shown that three out of four criminals were returned to jail. Winston tried to humanize the institutions by reducing time in solitary confinement, arranging lectures and concerts for inmates, and improving aftercare for discharged prisoners. He also began a classification system to separate political, first-time, and hard-core offenders. Political prisoners had the fewest personal restrictions. Convinced that "people should get what they deserved," Winston upheld capital punishment. Yet he admitted that his task of advising the king about whether a particular execution should be stayed was his most difficult job. How could he know when life imprisonment might be the crueler punishment?

During his time at the Home Office, Winston saw the labor legislation he had proposed while at the Board of Trade finally pass into law. But at the same time he lost the support of labor and trade unions for using troops to break a railway strike that had threatened to cripple the nation. Although some of the public thought this use of troops against civilians extreme, only months earlier other public voices had criticized him for not using enough force in settling a miners' strike in Wales. Winston was learning that someone would always think he'd made the wrong decision.

The year 1911 was brightened by two events. Members

of Parliament were granted a £400-a-year salary, effectively opening the House of Commons to the middle and working classes, and Winston's son was born. To no one's surprise, the boy was named Randolph.

Yet the other cares of state persisted. The question of home rule for Ireland created particular headaches in Parliament because of the problems of assuring the rights of Protestant Ulster in what would be a predominantly Catholic country. While Irish Nationalists cried that it would mean the mutilation of Ireland, Winston favored excluding Ulster from the new nation, especially since the Ulstermen didn't particularly want to be included in it. Negotiations proceeded as both sides armed; civil war seemed ever more likely.

Winston's other constant nightmare was the suffragettes. Early in his career he'd remarked about the folly of giving votes to women, and ever since he'd been a favorite target of the feminists' fury. Groups of suffragettes would show up at his meetings to jeer and heckle; besides embarrasing a prominent and powerful man, they received good publicity, for Winston's speeches were always well attended by the press. Winston first refused to answer the women's questions simply because they were not party concerns. Then, exasperated by their repeated disturbances, he tried to ignore them. Although he swore that he would not be "henpecked" on the issue and that nothing would induce him to give women the vote, he still offered to pay their fines when they were arrested. For Winston did not oppose women's suffrage in principle; he worried about the political aspects of the franchise. Under existing laws, only propertied women would have the right to vote, and this would almost certainly give the Conservatives a clear majority. How could any right-thinking Liberal support such a move?

Added to these dilemmas was the threat of German aggression. In July 1911, Germany sent warships to Agadir, Morocco, to assert claims to that land. Winston, who had previously attended military maneuvers in Germany without a second thought, suddenly saw the Kaiser and his well-equipped army in a more sinister light. Realizing that as home secretary he was also in charge of national security, Winston started writing scenarios for war. He drafted a prophetic memo about the probable course of a European conflict and began complaining that Britain was not at all prepared to fight. His voice grew so strong and so urgent that by the fall he was made first lord of the Admiralty.

Winston, the onetime soldier, now had the entire British navy to command. Following his hero Napoleon's advice that to have peace you must prepare for war, Winston turned the Admiralty upside down. He set up a Naval War Staff to advise and oversee operations and increased secret service activities. Each morning he charted the movements of the German fleet on a big map in his office to keep his staff ever mindful that an attack might come any day. Abandoning all talk of military reductions, he demanded more funds for ships and arms. New larger guns graced sleek new battleships driven by oil rather than less efficient coal. He also improved wages and conditions for seamen, a move that made him more popular below deck than above. While intellectually unable to believe in a war between "two civilized European nations," Winston was taking no chances.

Convinced of the important role of airplanes in any future action, Winston created the Royal Naval Air Service in 1912 and urged the development of antiaircraft guns. He even took flying lessons himself, going up in almost every kind of contraption until his instructor's crash and Clementine's nightmares convinced him to stop. He couldn't have gotten his pilot's license anyway. No one was willing to let him go up alone; he was too important, and the risk was too great.

Winston's plans were costly. Parliamentary resistance to his budgets grew each year, and by 1914 even Lloyd George begged him to cut back. But resistance ended that summer. In late June the Archduke Francis Ferdinand was assassinated in Sarajevo, and a European war seemed inevitable.

In July Winston called a test mobilization of the fleet and pressed the cabinet for permission to call a full mobilization in August. He got no response. Still feeling that "everything tends towards catastrophe and collapse," he put the Medi-

terranean fleet on alert. As sabers rattled across the Continent, and women everywhere started Red Cross classes, Winston waited for his orders. Taking his family on a short holiday, he played in the sand with his children, showing them how to build fortresses and dikes. He was in a wonderful mood. While he deplored its horrors, he loved the romance and heroics of war. "I am interested, geared up, and happy," he confided to his wife. "Is it not horrible to be built like that?"

When Germany moved against Russia on August 1, Winston decided to wait no longer. Hoping for retrospective approval, he sent England's ships into the North Sea. The next day German guns aimed at Belgium, whose neutrality had been guaranteed by an Anglo-German treaty. Britain issued an ultimatum to its former ally: withdraw your forces or prepare to fight.

On August 4 Germany invaded Belgium. Now Britain would be at war. That evening Winston made his way to his office through streets jammed with excited people. At 11 P.M. the ultimatum expired, and Winston telegraphed his waiting ships: "Commence hostilities against Germany." Outside his window the crowds began to sing "God Save the King."

*Churchill (left) in the uniform of first lord of the Admiralty*

# MINISTER

# 5

General Kitchener would one day remind Winston that there was one thing no one could ever take away from him: "The Fleet was ready."

Actually, that fleet eager for action in the North Sea was far from ready. They only believed they were. Guns, mines, and torpedoes were in short supply, and these inadequacies became painfully apparent once the euphoria of the start of the war had passed. Several British ships went down in the North Sea, and two big German warships escaped to the comparative quiet of the Eastern Mediterranean, where they enjoyed the protection of their newly declared ally Turkey. The British public, expecting to feast on victories, found themselves faced with a diet of defeats and disappointments.

Although not entirely responsible for the progress of the war, Winston took most of the blame. Yet he refused to be discouraged. While the private man admitted that war was "vile and wicked folly and barbarism," the public man radiated courage and confidence. "When all looked black and spirits were inclined to droop," remembered one colleague, "he could not only see, but compel others to see, the brighter side of the picture."

Youth and vitality were not enough to carry Winston's job, however. The first lord of the Admiralty also had to be a good manager, and administration had never been one of Winston's strengths. He saw himself as a second Napoleon; he wanted to command. Consulting and conferring with advisers made him restless and edgy. Admiralty colleagues soon resented his insensitivity to their opinions, as well as his habit of asking them to approve past, instead of future actions.

His second-in-command, the aged Admiral Lord Fisher, did little to smooth matters. Winston had chosen for first sea lord as strong a man as himself, and one who was just as determined to run the department. Very quickly, the two worked out an uneasy truce simply by avoiding each other. Lord Fisher worked the day shift, arriving at and leaving the office early. Winston came late and stayed on until very early in the morning, when he went home to sleep. It became his practice to wake up at 8 A.M. and then work in bed for a couple of hours propped up on huge pillows with an enormous cigar in his mouth. Brightly colored dispatch boxes littered the bedclothes, and a stenographer perched at the foot of the bed. His absorption in the matters at hand was complete, his concentration in that bustling room perfect, and, as his secretary noted, his "disregard of time . . . sublime—he firmly believes that it waits for him."

As summer wore into autumn, Winston saw the pages of his 1911 memorandum come to life. Belgium fell into German hands, and U-boats lurked in northern waters. Winston paced his office in frustration. He wanted to be in the show himself, not merely directing it from the dark side of the footlights. He soon found a way of doing so.

Winston's first intervention in the war came to be known as the "Dunkirk Circus." He had already established an aircraft base at the French town of Dunkirk on the English Channel, which was protected by a brigade of Royal Marines who traveled about in a fleet of specially adapted Rolls-

Royces. As a diversionary measure to perplex and worry the Germans, Winston landed a mixed force of marines and soldiers there in September. This special group did little besides parade, but Winston was thrilled to be moving real soldiers about at last. The prime minister was not thrilled, however, and the operation shut down quickly and quietly.

Winston's second involvement seemed no less ridiculous to the public. By early October the Belgian army had retreated as far as Antwerp. With one more push the city would fall to the Germans, leaving the way clear for a German advance to the Channel coast. The Belgians called on Britain for help. Winston sent a brigade of marines, and then was himself dispatched by Kitchener (his opposite number for the army) to go to Antwerp and convince the defenders of the city to hold on until more reinforcements arrived.

Dressed in a quasi-official uniform, Winston set up headquarters in Antwerp's finest hotel and proceeded to order about the Belgian king, ministers, soldiers, and sailors as if he were in his own office. The situation reminded one observer of "a scene in a melodrama where the hero dashes up bare-headed on a foam-flecked horse, and saves the heroine, or the old homestead, or the family fortune, as the case may be." Winston certainly behaved dramatically. Within a few days he had coordinated all troop movements, wired home for two more naval brigades, and even offered to resign his Admiralty position in order to command British troops in Belgium. He even went so far as to suggest his successor. Kitchener was taken with the idea, and thought he might find Winston a commission. The rest of the cabinet thought he'd gone mad, however, and ordered him home at once, mollifying him by pointing out that his department had been deprived of his leadership for a week.

Antwerp fell within hours of Winston's departure. Twenty five hundred men were killed or captured in the fighting.

Despite the fact that Winston's presence had delayed the fall of the city long enough for the British to make sure that their forces in Belgium were not cut off from their supply lines, the first lord was ridiculed and criticized for his amateur theatrics, his apparent lack of concern for the navy, and his "meddling." The public thought the whole thing was Winston's flamboyant idea. From now on, he should stay behind the footlights.

Although his Antwerp adventure had weakened his reputation and authority, Winston was thrilled by his heroic gestures. "This, this is living history!" he exclaimed to a friend at dinner one evening. "Everything we are doing and saying is thrilling—it will be read by a thousand generations, think of that! Why, I would not be out of this glorious delicious war for anything the world could give me."

His companion's eyes widened. Delicious? A ten-mile-wide stretch of land now reached from the English Channel to the Swiss border on which no trees grew, no animals grazed, no houses stood, and no children played. Corpses and fresh graves dotted the landscape. On either side of this hellish wasteland warrenlike trenches sheltered frightened, mud-soaked soldiers from the deafening shower of shells that were fired by an unseen enemy in an opposite trench. The armies were deadlocked with no hope of release. How could he say "delicious"?

But Winston had the soul of a soldier. For him all action was exciting. He'd had a marvelous time in Antwerp and looked forward to more time at the front.

By December 1914, however, Winston realized that a second front would have to be opened if the Allies were to win the war. The soldiers in France were merely "chewing barbed wire." Neither side had the strength to penetrate the other's lines. But a surprise attack from another quarter might give them the advantage they needed.

Tentatively, Winston proposed a naval attack on the Dardanelles, a narrow straight connecting the Aegean Sea and the Sea of Marmara. By using Britain's greatest strength, its navy, the Allies could defeat Turkey, and use that country as a base of operations for an eastern attack on Germany. Winston knew that ships couldn't do it alone; heavy bombardment would have to be part of the plan, as would infantry. But it just might work. The commander of the Aegean Fleet had agreed it was possible, and a trial barrage in November had damaged Turkish forts at the tip of the Gallipoli Peninsula. Eager to get the navy into the midst of war strategy, Winston believed his plan could succeed. Besides, how could one expect victory without risk?

The sea lords and the cabinet first dismissed Winston's ideas as unpractical. But in January 1915 Russia asked for British help in deflecting Turkish pressure on the Caucasus Mountains. Suddenly Winston's plans didn't seem so lunatic. Perhaps, while helping the Russians, a British show of strength could persuade the neutral Balkan nations to help the Allies break the deadlock on the Western Front.

Now the plans went forward without obstacle. According to Admiralty estimates, losses of men and matériel would be negligible. The big ships with their fifteen-inch guns would have no trouble keeping out of Turkish range, and the others in the fleet were old and expendable. Best of all, if things started going badly, the attack could be stopped at any time and explained away as a "demonstration"; and if the plan worked, troops could be in Constantinople in a matter of days. There seemed to be nothing to lose, and everything to gain.

No one ever said "this is ridiculous; ships can't take land." Kitchener and Fisher were uneasy and unsupportive, but the rest of the Admiralty War Council was enthusiastic. On January 13 they decided that "the Admiralty should prepare for a naval expedition in February to bombard and take the Gallipoli Peninsula with Constantinople as its objective."

Many of the sailors bound for the Eastern Mediterranean saw the whole thing as a romp. They packed Constantinople guide books with their uniforms and regaled each other with stories about how the Turks were especially vulnerable in night attacks because they were afraid of the dark. The government was equally optimistic, supplying each ship with a load of printed leaflets to distribute throughout the conquered city.

The romp turned quickly into a full-scale operation using

more than fifty ships and fifty thousand men. Bombardment began on February 19 but was stopped by storms until the 25th. It seemed to be going well, however. A few small landing parties had been able to finish off the guns guarding the entrance to the straits, and Winston was happy and excited over his apparent success.

His elation soon turned to distress, however, for the attack was proceeding too slowly. The current was always against them, and Turkish searchlights made night attacks impossible. The Turks had also mined the waters heavily, and the British had no minesweepers in their fleet. Worst of all, the commander who had been most supportive of the plan suffered a nervous breakdown and had to be sent home.

On March 18 a new bombardment began. This time the British knocked out the forts and started moving up the Dardanelles. A new area of mines along the coast frightened them off, however, and they retreated to the safety of the Aegean. The Turkish and German gunners at the forts couldn't believe their eyes. With less than a day's supply of ammunition left, they would have surrendered within hours had the Allies kept up their attack.

The retreat marked the turning point in the campaign. Kitchener finally agreed to send soldiers to Gallipoli, but lack of transport caused more delays. Winston fumed. Not only would the campaign be an army show from now on, but the Turks would surely use the time to rearm. The War Council denied his pleas for continued bombardment. Instead of fighting, British servicemen took sailing lessons and wrote poetry while the Turks strung barbed wire along their beaches.

When the British landed in Gallipoli in April it was the first time open boats had been used against defended beachheads in modern warfare. On the decks of the ships, commanders lowered their field glasses from their eyes. No one could bear to watch. The men were slaughtered as they landed. Dead and dying bodies clogged the shallow water, and later arrivals had to climb over struggling comrades to reach the shore.

The first reports to reach London were positive, but it was soon obvious that the Turks still held the high ground. Gallipoli was another no-man's-land. Demoralized soldiers wounded themselves rather than go back into battle. The cabinet and War Council were discouraged too. They denied Winston's request for a June renewal but approved an August landing, once more giving the Turks plenty of time to regroup.

This time England lost more than forty thousand men in three weeks. It was time to give up. The War Council recalled the flagship of the fleet and planned to bring the other ships home in October.

Winston by this time was no longer in power. He'd had to resign from the Admiralty in May 1915 when a new coalition replaced the government forced out of office by public outrage and cabinet dissension over Gallipoli. Winston was not out of office entirely; he managed the king's property in the Duchy of Lancaster, a cabinet post with very little responsibility, and retained his seat on the war department's policy-making Dardanelles Committee, but he could no longer direct or command.

For Winston had taken the full share of the blame for the Dardanelles disaster. While he really had no control over the insufficient manpower, the mines, the leaky ships, and the barbed wire that foiled his plans, many things were his fault. His proposal took no account of the weather, of the multiple problems of amphibious landings, of the real relationship between naval guns and land defense, or of the true extent of Turkish capabilities. Although he later insisted that other authorities had framed and approved the plans that he merely implemented, Winston was in large part behind the tragic mess.

And he paid dearly for it the rest of his life. Not only was he demoted to a post usually reserved for senile politicians, but he was also humiliated. The *Morning Post* called him a "danger and an anxiety to the nation." Party colleagues saw him as a threat to the Empire. Winston was shocked. He hadn't realized how much mistrust he'd inspired. Too busy with naval affairs, he'd neglected his duties in the House, and fellow members felt no qualms about deserting the man they felt had deserted *them.* Winston fell unmourned. Like his father, he'd been unaware of his plummeting reputation and oblivious to the true situation.

It seemed as if his brilliant career was at an end. The Duchy of Lancaster occupied two hours of his time a week. His lowered status on the Dardanelles Committee reduced his workload there, too. His secretary reported that Winston was like "Beethoven deaf," deprived of joy and livelihood at one blow.

His mood was not completely black, of course. Winston found a hobby to distract himself. One afternoon he watched his sister-in-law painting in the garden and decided it looked like fun. Borrowing his nephew's paint box, he experimented with brushes and colors and within a month purchased an entire kit of his own. Painting was his opiate. Now whenever he traveled, the paintbox and the dispatch box vied for space in his luggage.

Besides the support of his family and friends, Winston was heartened by the few brave voices that assured him that his time would come. And once he cheered himself considerably by reflecting that despite ten years in the cabinet, and five of them in high office, he was still the junior member by a good ten years.

But early in November 1915 the Dardanelles Committee disbanded, and a handpicked War Committee took over the evacuation. Unwilling to stay in a position of "well-paid inactivity," Winston resigned from the cabinet (but not from the Parliament) and reported to the army. Standing directly behind the spot where his father had made his resignation speech, Winston bade farewell to the House of Commons.

At age 41, Winston was again in uniform. Perhaps his father had been right, after all—perhaps that was all he was good for. Now he would find out. He would also see if his "star" still watched over him. If he was spared in France, as he had been in Cuba and Africa, then Winston would know

*Churchill (center), wearing his French helmet, was photographed with fellow soldiers in France in 1916.*

that his future held great and important things. And if he fell, well, what matter—the fates had obviously abandoned him anyway.

After serving an apprenticeship in the cold, wet, dangerous trenches, Winston took command of an infantry battalion of the Sixth Royal Scots Fusiliers. His first act was to gather his officers for an urgent conference. "War is declared, gentlemen," he said, looking about him, "on the lice!" Three days of strenuous scrubbing and laundering ensured Winston of a comfortable and cheerful battalion to lead.

No one stayed in the trenches all the time. Men had to be relieved every few days for a rest from the noise and tension of constant battle. On his duty days, Winston inspected the trenches three times daily, checking sandbags and sentries with equal attention. His blue steel French helmet, which he found superior to the English tin hat, soon became a familiar sight to the Fusiliers, and Winston's private luxuries—his cigars, private stock of liquor, tin bathtub, and pocket edition of Shakespeare—became the subjects of their good-natured ribbing. For Winston had won his men's affection from the start by making sure that distinguished visitors walked the trenches with him, even at the risk of scuffing their shiny boots in the mud or tearing their impeccable uniforms on the barbed wire.

Winston taught his men that war should be fought with good humor and grace. "Laugh a little, and teach your men to laugh," he told his officers. "War is a game that is played with a smile. If you can't smile, grin. If you can't grin, keep out of the way until you can."

In March 1916 Winston went back to London for a debate at the House of Commons. Alarmed at the divisiveness he saw in the government, he wondered if he might be needed more in England than in France. When his battalion merged with another shortly thereafter, Winston resigned his commission for the last time and, after finding posts for all his officers, returned to Parliament.

Once again Winston criticized and campaigned in Commons. One of his favorite themes was the greater use of Empire resources in the war effort. Indian and African soldiers should join the British on the field. Grimly, he reminded the Parliament, "nearly a thousand men—Englishmen, Britishers, men of our own race—are knocked into bundles of bloody rags every twenty-four hours, and carried away to hasty graves or field ambulances." Let others share the burden.

Winston also worked hard to restore his good name and his finances. Once again he turned to journalism. Thanks to a series of articles for the *London Magazine,* he was soon earning more than he had at the Admiralty. His reputation was helped when an investigative commission found the prime minister and the government more culpable than Winston for Gallipoli. Winston was still at fault, but now he shared the blame with some of the most eminent men in the country.

On the whole, however, it was not a happy time for him. An outsider to both parties, he had not held office for two years. He was "simply existing."

When Winston was asked to be minister of munitions in 1917, he was surprised at the complaints the appointment drew. Evidently his colleagues still didn't trust him. Even his family had mixed emotions about the job. "Stick to munitions," advised one aunt, "and don't try & run the govt!"

The twelve-thousand-member Ministry of Munitions was already a going concern when Winston took it over; he wouldn't be able to leave much of a mark there. From his headquarters at the Metropole Hotel in Trafalgar Square, Winston established a Munitions Council and Secretariat to handle the ministry's administrative details for him, and then devoted himself to increasing production and decreasing waste. Morning found him at his desk, but the afternoons were saved for jaunts to factories or to France to check on deliveries and the quality of ammunition and equipment.

Winston liked the job, admitting that "it is very pleasant to work with competent people." Although he seemed uncharacteristically cautious and subdued, he still occasionally took a hard line. When munitions workers grumbled about low wages, Winston declared that any striking laborer would immediately lose his draft deferment. Production continued undisturbed.

Winston complained that "chemists in spectacles" were ruining the romance of war, yet he was not about to turn his back on modern technology. He was more convinced than ever that airplanes were essential for victory, and he also suggested the design for tanks and pushed for their production and deployment. Only these huge caterpillar vehicles could restore mobility to the Western Front.

Winston's management also helped the other weapon he felt necessary to win the war—the American army. So many Doughboy divisions were supplied with British munitions in 1917 that General John J. Pershing gave Winston a medal.

In his speeches in Commons, Winston continued to inspire and encourage his countrymen. His words gave them the strength to hang on through the grief, terror, and enormous physical hardships of the war. In April 1918, as the war drew to its bloody close, Winston cited Britons as the source of British strength:

> No demand is too novel or too sudden to be met. No need too unexpected to be supplied. No strain too prolonged for the patience of our people. No suffering or peril daunts their hearts. Instead of quarreling, giving way as we do from time to time to moods of pessimism and of irritation, we ought to be thankful that if such truths and dangers were destined for our country, we are here to share them, and see them slowly and surely overcome.

On the morning of November 11, 1918, Winston stood in his office staring out at Trafalgar Square. Clementine, heavily pregnant with their fourth child, stood beside him. As Big Ben tolled 11, people began pouring out of buildings to embrace and laugh and dance in the streets. The Churchills turned away from the window, silently made their way downstairs to the waiting car, and drove slowly to the prime minister's house to offer their congratulations. "I was conscious of reaction rather than elation," recalled Winston. The crowd, however, was delirious; some people even climbed on the roofs of their cars to shout and wave their flags. The war was over.

# CHANCELLOR

# 6

The war in Europe might have been over, but the battles in Britain were just beginning.

A post-war general election (that for the first time in British history included all adult males and propertied women over the age of thirty) returned the Liberal coalition to power. But the Liberal Party itself was splitting into Liberal and Labour factions. And the Conservatives had gained many more seats in the House of Commons. The new government would not run smoothly.

Britain was changed too. Nearly a million men had died in the war. Their grieving survivors wanted nothing more than a "return to normalcy," the remembered peace and prosperity of the years before 1914. But no one, not even prime ministers, can turn back the clock. The postwar world was chaotic, filled with aftershocks and unrest as people discovered that the jobs, the friends, and sometimes even the homes they'd known were gone forever.

Winston Churchill, chubby and balding at 44, now became secretary of state for War and Air. Politically, he was no more secure. His comparative youth, ambition, energy, flamboyance, and renown were still suspect to the traditionally reserved men he had to work with. While no one denied his intelligence, eloquence, and infinite capacity for hard work, very few were yet willing to trust him.

The people who trusted him most—his family—rarely saw him. Winston's four children—Diana, Randolph, Sarah, and Marigold—knew him more as an occasional playmate than as a father. One of the children's favorite games was "Bear," which decades later Randolph could still describe from a young boy's excited perspective:

> Father was the Bear. We had to turn our backs and close our eyes and he would climb a tree. All us children . . . had then to go and look for Bear. We were very much afraid but would advance courageously on a tree and say: "Bear! Bear! Bear!" And then run away. Suddenly he would drop from a tree and we would scatter in various directions. He would pursue us and the one he caught would be the loser.

Such interludes were rare. Most days found Winston in the War Office instead of the garden. His first priority was to develop an equitable plan for demobilizing the army. Once the Armistice had been signed, everyone wanted to come home at once. The first ones back, after all, would have the best shot at jobs and homes. The problem was the men were still needed on the front until the terms of the peace treaty were set. Winston's solution was to let three out of every four soldiers go, and to pay that fourth man double to stay on until a volunteer could take his place. Under his supervision, daily military expenditure fell from £4 million in January 1919 to £1.25 million that September. The army was literally melting away.

While disbanding the army, Winston was also securing the future of the Royal Air Force as a separate service, albeit one without equipment, because he believed air power the most efficient defense for the Empire. But for the most part he took up his old cause of reducing military spending. He even insisted that military estimates be computed on the prediction that Britain would not be engaged in any great war in the next ten years. Eager for that magic "return to normalcy," the cabinet agreed to this, never questioning how anyone could assume such a thing. As a result, Winston oversaw a skeleton army and munitions factories that slowly turned to other things. By the early 1930s, Britain had no armaments industry to speak of.

It would have been strange for a war-weary nation to adopt any other policy than disarmament. Certainly the government pursued it faithfully. But Winston felt there should be exceptions to the rule and soon found himself in a cabinet conflict once more.

This time the crisis was in Russia, which by the end of the war had become the scene of civil wars, revolution, and counterrevolutions. Lenin and his Bolshevik cohorts held Moscow and nearby provincial capitals, but their grasp was weak. Anti-Bolshevik forces, aided by British men and arms, threatened their precarious power from the outer provinces.

But in 1919 Britain had lost its taste for helping other nations. There'd been enough fighting. Winston, whose personal ideology, loyalty to a former ally, and conviction that the Bolsheviks would not cooperate with any Western alliance made him a fervent anti-Communist, asked for men and matériel to fight Lenin, a man he'd once compared to "a plague bacillus." At the very least he wanted a clear decision as to whether the government was going to "wind up the Russian operations or to press them with vigor." This was a decision none of the Allies, not even the United States, seemed able to make.

The cabinet finally decided to offer the anti-Bolsheviks money and arms but not men. Disgusted that they were leaving the Russians to "murder each other without let or hindrance," Winston nevertheless evacuated the remaining British soldiers. At the same time, however, he called for a small volunteer force to cover the withdrawal, and the press immediately accused him both of making secret deals with the Russians and of trying to start a new war. Denied outside support, the anti-Bolshevik armies soon collapsed, and the Union of Soviet Socialist Republics took over the vast territory that had once been Russia. In 1929 Winston was to observe sadly that the country "had been frozen in an indefinite winter of subhuman doctrine and superhuman tyranny."

Given the climate of the times, it is not at all odd that by early 1921 Winston was the head of a war department with no wars to fight. His ever-shrinking duties offered no challenge or outlet for his talents. He wanted more action and greater responsibilities.

He got them in February 1921 when he became secretary of state for the colonies and had the entire British Empire to preserve and protect. One of his first tasks was to solve the problems caused by Indian immigration to Africa. Winston attempted to defuse the racial tensions building there by strictly limiting the number of immigrants and denying them land. He justified his decision by stating that "the democratic principles of Europe are by no means suited to the development of Asiatic and African people," and then turned the whole matter over to the care of the undersecretaries.

For Winston saw far more pressing problems within his purview. One was the future of British influence in the Middle East. Seeking to secure British supremacy at minimum expense, Winston established a Middle East Department within the Colonial Office to coordinate the duties of the War, India, Colonial and Foreign offices. With the advice and guidance of T. E. Lawrence, the legendary Lawrence of Arabia who had rallied Arab forces during the war, he called a conference in Cairo to devise and detail new policy.

In March 1921 Winston cheerfully packed his bags and boxes for the trip to Egypt. Fresh from the success of a show of his paintings in Paris (displayed under the pseudonym of Charles Morin), he stuck his paint box in with his shirts and ties. He fully intended "to paint a few pictures in the intervals between settling my business, and naturally I am taking all the right kinds of colors for the yellow desert, purple rocks, and crimson sunsets."

The business Winston went to settle was mainly the replacement of British land forces in the area with British aircraft and the establishment of states, and rulers, sympathetic to British interests. One critic dismissed his ideas as "hot air, aeroplanes, and Arabs," yet Winston prevailed. Within its first two days, the conference created two new nations: Iraq, once called Mesopotamia, and Transjordania, now called Jordan. Their pro-British kings were to administer these territories and the Royal Air Force was to protect them.

Winston's plans did not please everyone. The British government had already declared itself in favor of the creation of a Jewish national homeland in Palestine; the presence of Transjordania compromised that pledge. To keep peace, Winston had to assure the Arabs of British friendship and reassure the Jews by declaring that "personally, my heart is full of sympathy for Zionism." A year later he was still wobbling on the tightrope. In a White Paper he affirmed the "principle of a Jewish state but not the imposition of Jewish nationality on Palestinians" and managed to confuse and infuriate both Arabs and Jews at the same time.

With British planes flying over Iraqi skies, Winston could turn his full attention to the Irish troubles, which had simmered all through the war. The Nationalists had declared themselves the Republic of Ireland and elected a Parliament, even though they were technically still part of Britain. While secretary of war, Winston had advocated military force to reassert British rule and to subdue those who thought murder and violence would ensure independence. He had even created special forces trained to fight terror with terror. The most notorious of these were the ex-soldiers dressed in surplus khaki uniforms and black belts known as the Black and Tans.

British military victory in Ireland seemed impossible by 1921, and Colonial Secretary Churchill stopped demanding negotiation from strength and urged negotiation from truce instead. In December 1921 the Irish Parliament reluctantly accepted a treaty that granted them some degree of self-government while safe-guarding English interests. The six northern counties remained British, not Irish. Officially, the Irish question was answered.

But it had been answered by Irish ministers who were under threat of continued violence from British ministers who agreed to talk only when military victory was impossible. The treaty was signed but not accepted. Irish supporters and opponents split, and southern Ireland, delivered from a war with England, found itself in the midst of a bloody civil war.

The year that had begun so brightly for Winston ended in darkness privately as well as publicly. In June his mother (who in 1918 had married again, this time a man three years Winston's junior) died of complications following a broken leg. Loss of his mother was followed by the more tragic loss of his youngest child, Marigold, who sickened and died within one August week.

To ease his grief, Winston tried to lose himself in his work. The Irish question took most of his waking hours, and he filled the few that remained with writing the war memoirs that would ultimately be published as the six volume *The World Crisis*. "I cannot help getting very interested in the work," he admitted. "It is a great chance to put my whole case in an agreeable form to an attentive audience."

It was also a great chance to improve the Churchill finances. They were once again living in a state of "impecunious affluence." Another daughter, Mary, had been born after Marigold's death; another child and the social demands of cabinet office sorely taxed their budget. He had inherited little from his mother for the once wealthy heiress left a total estate of only £2,280. And while Winston had received an Irish manor called Garron Towers from a childless cousin, land cannot pay the tailor.

The new year brought no relief. The Turks went to war with the Greeks, and only a handful of Allied soldiers kept Turkey from overrunning Asia Minor and, more important, crossing the Dardanelles to Europe. The British cabinet resolved to resist the Turks at all costs, even at the risk of another war, for Turkish occupation of the Gallipoli Peninsula, a neutral zone since the war, would negate all the Allies had fought for there.

Winston compounded an already alarming situation by asking Commonwealth nations (former colonies now allied with Britain) for support in the event of military action. The French and Italians, who were by treaty supposed to be notified of any military move, read of this request in their morning papers. Commoners and diplomats alike were frightened and enraged by the government's bellicosity. But so were the Turks, who meekly retreated from the paper tiger. Winston's war never happened.

The damage had already been done, however. The Conservatives were furious; Britain was not to be the world's police force. The party rebelled against the coalition and forced the government to resign.

In the ensuing election the Conservatives won an overwhelming majority, while Coalition supporters met with almost universal defeat. Most conspicuous among them was Winston Churchill. Still recovering from an emergency appendectomy that coincided with the government's fall, he had made very few campaign appearances, and those he did make were marked by boos and catcalls. His defeat was spectacular. "In the twinkling of an eye," he wrote, "I found myself without an office, without a seat, without a party, and," he added, "without an appendix."

Winston lost his next two races as well. To take his mind off his string of defeats, he kept working on *The World Crisis*. With the royalties and the proceeds from the sale of the Irish property, he bought an Elizabethan manor house near London called Chartwell. He hoped to make a dream come true for Clementine who had once confided that "if only we could get a little country Home within our means and live there within our means it would add great happiness and peace to our lives." Winston heard only "country Home" and not "within our means," for he had to spend three times the purchase price just to make Chartwell habitable. And when the

renovation work was done, he began a series of beautifica-tion projects (including an artificial lake and a swimming pond) that cost another fortune.

His enforced leisure also gave him plenty of time to reconsider his political allegiance. He still dreamed of a Cen-tre Party to unite all anti-socialists under one progressive, liberal banner. But he knew now that it was impossible, espe-cially since after 1923 he no longer considered himself a Liberal. That party was now too much allied with the growing Labour faction. To Winston, Labour meant socialism and socialism meant Bolshevism. He had no choice but to return to the Conservative fold if he wanted to continue in poli-tics.

He had to return slowly, however, or lose his credibility altogether. Gently, he approached Conservative leaders about a seat. They helped him run in the next election as a self-made "Constitutionalist," something not quite Conserva-tive, yet Tory enough to attract support. He lost by only eight votes, and in 1924 ran, and won, as the Conservative candi-date for Epping. It was, he said, "just like coming home."

Not only was he back in Parliament but back in office, too. This time he held the spot second only to that of the prime minister, chancellor of the Exchequer. This was the office his father had held at the height of his career, and the one Winston had coveted since his schooldays.

It was not an easy time to take over the Treasury. Shrink-ing markets and rising production costs had led to massive unemployment, and dislocations in international trade had triggered a world-wide depression. Adding to the difficulties was Winston's real lack of financial expertise. He could bare-

*Winston, with his wife,
Clementine, on his return
from a financial conference
during his tenure as
chancellor of the Exchequer*

ly manage his personal budget. While he did know more than his father (Randolph had once asked the meaning of those "damned decimal dots"), he still lacked the understanding and imagination of an economist. Nor was he politically strong enough to set and follow his own course.

Consequently, Winston was forced to rely exclusively on the advice of experts. And almost all the experts agreed that the only hope for the British economy lay in returning to pre-war conditions. That meant reducing tariffs and stabilizing the currency by reverting to the gold standard. Winston was given other rules to follow as well. The budget always had to be balanced, income taxes had to be lowered, and a sinking fund had to be provided by raising new taxes and decreasing spending.

Winston's first budget, presented in a two-and-a-half-hour speech in Commons in 1925, attempted to meet all these conditions. He slashed military spending in order to have more money for social programs; he lowered the income tax rate but offset the loss with other new taxes; he proposed very few tariffs; and he tied the pound to gold. Had he not, currency would have been devalued more each year, and London would have declined as the financial capital of the world.

The upper-class experts insisted that the benefits of the gold standard would far outweigh its disadvantages. The working classes saw it differently. To keep their prices competitive, manufacturers had to reduce costs, and the only way to do that was to reduce wages. When coal-mine owners offered the miners seven hours' wages for eight hours' work, the miners knew the time had come for action. They threatened a strike and promised to take other workers out with them.

Rather than cripple the nation with a general strike, Winston tried to buy time by subsidizing the coal industry with several new taxes. But in May 1926 time, and money, ran out. The miners struck, and union printers soon followed, refusing to set the type for the *Daily Mail*'s editorial "For King and Country." The next day the rest of organized labor put down their tools. All over England factories were dark and quiet; trains and buses sat empty at their platforms. Civilian volunteers took over essential services, despite threats of violence from the strikers, just to keep the country going. One of them was Winston.

The chancellor of the Exchequer did more than prepare contingency plans for the strike. He also took over the press, publishing a government organ, the *British Gazette.* Winston used it more for propaganda than for information, filling the pages with patriotic poetry, innuendo, and anti-union statements. His aim was to break the strike and its threat to constitutional government in any way he could. His result was an everlasting monument to the horrors of state-controlled journalism.

The general strike, and the *Gazette,* both ended quickly. The miners' strike continued through the fall when, cold and hungry, the men put on their helmets and climbed down the shafts. No one had won anything. The disruption in coal production, however, affected other industries and compounded the nation's economic problems. Winston tried to keep up with the constant deficit by borrowing from one fund to fill another and became known as the "merriest tax collector since Robin Hood" because of the novelty of the items he tried to tax. (One of the most unsuccessful was his tax on bookmakers' bets.) Still, he could do no more than hold the line. Economic recovery would not be his to give.

Nor would his government give it either. The British public turned the Conservatives out of office in 1929. Winston kept his seat, but the newly elected Labour government had no use for him.

Winston would once again have time to paint, to finish the brick wall he was laying at Chartwell, to visit with his family, to see his friends, to study radio broadcasting, to read, and to write. It would be ten years before he held office again.

# PROPHET

## 7

With no pressing business to attend to, Winston decided to travel. In the fall of 1929 he set out on a trans-American tour with his brother, son, and nephew. Crossing Canada by train to the Pacific, the quartet spent a few days in California (where they met several movie stars) before heading back to Washington, where Winston met President Herbert Hoover.

The trip was not purely recreational. Winston had pulled together a large sum of money that he wanted his friend Bernard Baruch (whom he called "the greatest speculator that has ever been") to invest in American securities for him. On September 29 he wrote to Clementine that he'd already made a great deal of money that "must not be frittered away but kept for investment."

He never had a chance to do either. Winston was at the New York Stock Exchange that Black Tuesday when the market crashed, and he watched brokers scurrying about the trading floor like ants "in a disturbed ant-heap, offering each other enormous blocks of securities." Later that day he saw a man throw himself out a window. He might have considered such action himself, for the Crash wiped out most of his investment.

Yet money soon found its way back into Winston's pockets. He published his autobiography; he wrote weekly articles; he inherited money from a friend, he became a director of two coal companies; he sold his forthcoming family history, *Marlborough: His Life and Times,* to British publishers, and then sold both the American and serial rights as well; and he earned £10,000 for writing a screenplay for a film that was never produced. He even turned disaster into cash. When knocked down by a taxi in New York City in 1931, Winston wrote of the adventure while still in his hospital bed and sold it for $2,500.

Winston traveled to Europe, too, in those years. In 1932 he went to Bavaria to research the Marlborough book and consult with military experts about his campaigns. He saw more in Germany than battlefields, however. In this country that was not supposed to rearm after the war, he saw a surprising number of civilian flying clubs, which reminded him of a giant secret air force, and, even more alarming, "bands of sturdy Teutonic youths, marching through the streets and roads of Germany, with the light of desire in their eyes to suffer for their Fatherland."

When in England, however, Winston concentrated on politics. In 1931 Britain's ever-worsening economic situation forced Labour to make room for some Conservatives at the top. This new National, or coalition, government called on the ablest men of both parties to undertake the unpopular but essential economy measures needed to set Britain straight. But Winston was not among them. He had quarreled with his party over tariffs and colonial affairs, and although he endorsed the idea of a coalition cabinet, he had publicly referred to the Labour prime minister as a "boneless wonder." No surprise, then, that no office could be found for him.

But he was still caught up in the major debates of the decade. One of the biggest and bitterest issues was that of Indian independence. The Conservative government had reaffirmed an earlier promise of eventual self-rule for the subcontinent in 1929, but many Englishmen, as well as the Indian leaders Jawaharlal Nehru and Mahatma Gandhi, were now demanding a whole new commitment to self-government.

Winston opposed self-rule for a variety of reasons. He feared fierce racial and religious dissension in the country with the withdrawal of Britain's soothing hand, and he warned that no one government could hope to rule all of India's masses fairly. He railed against any negotiations with Gandhi, whom he described as an ex-prisoner "now posing as a fakir." Most of all as an ardent imperialist, Winston objected to the loss of any part of the British Empire, which was what self-government would mean. Once more refusing to follow the official line, Winston resigned from his party jobs to form committees, write articles, and give lectures to mobilize public opinion against independence. But he was standing on the wrong side of the fence. Faced with mounting pressures at home and in India, the cabinet had no alternative but to draft new plans for self-rule.

Winston's campaign had little effect on the course of events in India, but its effects on his own career were spectacular. His views made him very unpopular among his colleagues of both parties. Nor did his behavior help. In Commons he was rude, gossipy, and fidgety when others spoke on the issue, and his own speeches betrayed a fair amount of misinformation and prejudice. Unwilling to be embarrassed by him any longer, his fellow M.P.'s turned their backs to him, discounting all his proposals as self-serving drivel. With no allies and no political base, Winston had no hope of ever holding office again. At 60, his ministerial career seemed over.

Political exile didn't stop him from championing other causes, however. He urged British neutrality in the Spanish Civil War, mainly because "neither of these Spanish factions expresses our conception of civilization." And in 1936 when King Edward VIII decided he would rather marry a twice-divorced American woman than continue as king, Winston suggested that perhaps it was the puritanical government, rather than the king, that should abdicate—and then was shocked by the hostility his words provoked. The mantle of foolishness and irresponsibility was now firmly fastened about his shoulders.

So damaged was his reputation that, like the little boy who cried "wolf," no one believed him when he began warning of a very real and very grave danger. The martial spirit he had noted in Germany in 1932 had taken on frightening overtones the next year when Adolf Hitler came to power. "We watch with surprise and distress," he said, "the tumultuous insurgence of ferocity and war spirit, the pitiless ill-treatment of minorities, the denial of the normal predictions of civilized society to large numbers of individuals solely on the grounds of race." He was also alarmed by the German drive to rearm and cautioned that Britain's air force was not nearly strong enough to withstand a German attack. In speech after speech he urged money for arms, for training, and for research.

Once again his was the voice crying in the wilderness. While not advocating pacifism, the government still had no intention of spending anything more on munitions; in fact, their goal was disarmament. Britain would be secure with its European allies ran the official argument.

Winston saw that as a sad fantasy. "The removal of the just grievances of the vanquished ought to precede the disarmament of the victors," he declared. But no one was ready to deal with Hitler's grievances, just or unjust. German occupation of the Rhineland seemed to prove Winston's point, for suddenly a few more people began to hear the wolf clawing at the door. Pressing his advantage, Winston began lobbying for the reestablishment of the Ministry of Munitions. Unofficially supplied by government officials acting privately, with better facts and figures than those the Cabinet had, and supported by a handful of M.P.'s, Winston continued to warn that Nazism was "the greatest danger and emergency in our history."

The government, believing that the national mood was peaceful instead of bellicose, and wanting to stay in power, made only feeble attempts to improve Britain's defenses. But when Hitler continued his creeping conquest of Europe by annexing Austria in 1938, it became obvious to everyone that something more would have to be done. Winston proposed a grand British-French-Russian alliance to protect European peace. Neville Chamberlain, the prime minister, preferred direct negotiations with Germany.

At a meeting in Munich in 1938, Hitler demanded the cession of the German-speaking territories in Czechoslovakia. Chamberlain, haunted by the ghosts of the millions of young men who had died in the first world war, agreed to the dictator's demands rather than risk another bloodbath. After signing the agreement that dismembered a sovereign state, he flew home to England proudly proclaiming "peace in our time."

Winston immediately attacked the treaty. In a parliamentary speech he pointed out that Britain's own safety now depended on German goodwill. He ended with these chilling words:

Do not suppose that this is the end. This is only the beginning of the reckoning. This is only the first step, the first foretaste of a bitter cup which will be proferred to us year by year unless by a supreme recovery of our moral health and martial vigor, we arise again and take our stand for freedom as in the olden time.

Winston was right. Hitler was still hungry. In March 1939 the German armies claimed the rest of Czechoslovakia, and the prophet saw his words come true. Suddenly the government was with him. Now Britain guaranteed aid to Poland, Greece, and Rumania in case of Nazi attack; now the Ministry of Supply took shape; now air-raid drills were common practice; and now, for the first time in English history, a peacetime draft swelled the army.

But the government still would not find a place for Winston in its ranks, no matter how the press and public clamored for his inclusion. Alone, he tried to arrange the Grand Alliance, but only France would agree. Russia chose instead to sign a nonaggression pact with Germany, which promised, in short, that the two would not wage war against each other.

That was all Hitler needed. He immediately demanded the cession of Poland, so that Germany's borders would meet Russia's. The Polish government refused to consider it. Secure in the knowledge that his actions would be unopposed from the East, in the early morning of September 1, 1939, Hitler sent his armies into Poland and World War II.

Bound by treaty to aid Poland, Britain would have to fight. That afternoon Chamberlain asked Winston to join a war cabinet. Two days later, war was formally declared. Within minutes, sirens wailed the first air-raid warnings. Picking up a bottle of brandy from the sideboard, Winston took Clementine by the arm and joined his fellow Londoners in the nearest shelter until the all-clear sounded. Then, leaving the brandy with his wife, he proceeded to the House of Commons for the noon debate.

He never got there. Secretaries intercepted him in the lobby and directed him to the prime minister's office, where Chamberlain offered him his old post as first lord of the Admiralty. Winston accepted graciously, then went home for lunch, opened a bottle of champagne for a victory toast, and took his usual nap. At 6 P.M. he was back in his Admiralty office. The news had already gone out to the fleet: "Winston is back."

The war began more with a whimper than a bang. For the first few months France and Britain sat and waited for Hitler's fury to spend itself on the Polish plains. Nor did they make any attempt to attack the German ships and U-boats that were sinking their vessels.

During this "phony war," Winston's popularity rose dramatically. His years of isolation and independence marked him as a leader who rose above the mistakes and deficiencies of the coalition, and now his vigor as first lord, as well as his frequent radio broadcasts, cemented his position. As Chamberlain's cabinet lost its needed support, Winston's lisping voice called for greater national unity and strength.

This unusual radio photo shows Churchill broadcasting a message to the United States in October 1939, urging America to join Great Britain in opposing Hitler's aggression.

"Let party interest be ignored," he urged. "Let all our energies be harnessed, let the whole ability and forces of the nation be hurled into the struggle, and let all the strong horses be pulling on the collar."

One bright day in May 1940 Winston reported that he felt as if "I were walking with destiny, and that all my past life has been but a preparation for this hour and for this trial." That morning Hitler had invaded France, Belgium, and Holland. Chamberlain had resigned, asking Winston to take his place. Winston Churchill was now prime minister.

Quickly assembling his cabinet (reserving the job of minister of defense for himself), Winston asked the members of the House of Commons for their approval and help. Declaring that he had nothing to offer but "blood, toil, tears, and sweat," he went on to describe Britain's commitment to victory:

> You ask, what is our policy? I will say: it is to wage war, by sea, land, and air, with all our might and with all the strength God can give us: to wage war against a monstrous tyranny, never surpassed in the dark, lamentable catalogue of human crime. That is our policy. You ask, what is our aim? I can answer in one word: victory—victory at all costs, victory in spite of all terror, victory, however long and hard the road may be; for without victory there is no survival.

# HERO

# 8

The new prime minister was sixty-five years old. Most of his contemporaries were retiring or dying instead of taking on the leadership of a nation at war. Winston was undaunted, however. He firmly believed that the challenge of the crisis would tap hidden reserves of strength and help him "rise to the height of the great occasion."

He attacked his duties with efficiency and urgency. He tolerated no delays and no excuses. Senior civil servants soon learned to run through the corridors about their business instead of strolling. Regular office hours, and weekends off, vanished from the schedules, and a series of late-night meetings, called the "Midnight Follies" by one secretary, became routine.

The boss worked as hard as the rest of the staff, although in his own style. Winston still worked in bed until 11, then got up, bathed, dressed, and went to his office. His morning ended at one with a large lunch that was invariably followed by champagne, port, brandy, and a cigar. He was back at his desk until "teatime"—a five o'clock whiskey and soda. A quick nap before he dressed for dinner got the prime minister through another heavy meal and a short game of backgammon with his wife. Only then did his working day really begin, and it continued almost until dawn. No more than seven hours' sleep and no fewer than fifteen cigars got Winston through his busy days.

The new government faced an immediate crisis in France. The German onslaught was pushing the Allied troops closer and closer to the sea. By the end of Winston's first month in office hundreds of thousands of British and French troops were stranded on the beaches of the English Channel near Dunkirk. Rather than let them be massacred, Britain rescued them. From every little port and harbor and river in southeastern England, civilians set out to save their countrymen. Sailboats, rowboats, paddleboats, tugboats, and coastal steamers made an unlikely flotilla that crossed and recrossed the choppy seas until more than 300,000 men had been carried to safety. Losses were high and the Germans still had France, yet all over England Dunkirk was hailed as a great victory.

Winston dampened England's exaltation by pointing out that wars are not won by evacuations and that Germany would certainly now attack Britain. But he tempered his gloomy prophecy with a rousing promise:

> We shall fight them on the beaches, we shall fight on the landing grounds, we shall fight in the hills; we shall never surrender, and even if, which I do not for a moment believe, this island or a large part of it were subjugated and starving, then our Empire beyond the seas, armed and guarded by the British Fleet, would carry on the struggle, until, in God's good time, the New World, with all its power and might, steps forth to the rescue and liberation of the old.

Winston's mention of the New World as savior of the Old was no mere rhetorical device. He knew that American support was essential for Allied victory and had opened correspondence with President Franklin Roosevelt shortly after taking office in the hope of getting much needed munitions.

The need became greater in late June when France surrendered to the Germans. Winston broadcast a new appeal to his people:

> The Battle of France is over. I expect that the Battle of Britain is about to begin. . . . Let us therefore brace ourselves to our duties, and so bear ourselves that, if the British Empire and Commonwealth last for a thousand years, men will still say: "This was their finest hour."

The Battle of Britain began in August, but in the air, not on the ground. Realizing that he would have to control the skies before he could safely land troops on the shores, Hitler sent wave after wave of Luftwaffe planes over the English Channel. Each time the outnumbered British pilots beat them back. Every available airman and flying machine went into action. By September 15, however, the Royal Air Force had reached the end of its reserves. There simply were no more planes.

But the Germans had come to their limit as well. They had lost far more aircraft than they had anticipated. Fearing that the British had as many planes left as they boasted they did, Hilter called off the operation. That night, Winston could tell the nation gratefully that "never in the field of human conflict has so much been owed by so many to so few."

A new horror soon replaced the old. That autumn German strategy switched from battle to blitz, and for fifty-seven consecutive nights a constant rain of bombs sent Londoners scurrying to the underground stations for safety. The Blitz was designed to terrorize the British into submission, but they refused to be terrorized. Much of their strength and spirit came from their prime minister. Wearing a shapeless one-piece coverall he called his "siren suit" and holding up two

*Prime Minister Winston Churchill tours Coventry Cathedral, which was destroyed in the Blitz.*

fingers in a "V-for-Victory" sign, he made daily visits to bombed-out factories, shops, playgrounds, and houses, often weeping with sorrow at the destruction and with pride at the courage of the people he met searching through the rubble for the ruined remnants of their lives. That Winston shared their suffering made it easier to bear.

He also comforted them with his words. He kept the House of Commons well informed of all war progress and made frequent radio broadcasts to the nation. People eagerly anticipated his next talk, despite his gravelly voice, his lisp, and his peculiar way of saying "Nazi" so that it came out "Narzi." He sent courage and confidence through the airwaves in speeches composed late at night as he paced his office in a crumpled dinner jacket and bedroom slippers, dropping cigar ash and whiskey on himself as he tried out the words he wanted. He told them it would be hard and horrible; and he told them they would prevail.

For almost a year Britain fought alone against Hitler. All the major cities, and even Buckingham Palace and the Houses of Parliament, were bombed, and more than 60,000 civilians lost their lives. Convinced that the island would give in soon, Hitler began planning an immense world capital at Berlin that would be far greater than St. Peter's in Rome. Yet the British refused to surrender. The short, fat man who led them did all he could to make sure that those buildings remained blueprints. By the spring, after eight months of demoralizing and exhausting bombing, Britain was still standing on her own, capable of defending herself in the air and on the sea. As Winston would later boast: "Alone, but upborne by every generous heart-beat of mankind, we had defied the tyrant in his hour of triumph."

In June 1941 Hitler stopped hammering at Britain's gates and turned his war machine on his Russian "ally." But he met no easy victory there either. Although no friend of the Communists or their leader, Stalin, Winston sent aid to these newest victims of Nazism, explaining that "if Hitler invaded Hell, I would at least make a favorable reference to the Devil in the House of Commons." In July he signed an Anglo-Soviet agreement not to make a separate peace with Germany and reminded both nations that

> we have but one aim and one single irrevocable purpose. We are resolved to destroy Hitler and every vestige of the Nazi regime. From this, nothing will turn us, nothing. We will never parley. We will never negotiate with Hitler or any of his gang. We shall fight him . . . until . . . we have rid the earth of his shadow. . . . We shall never surrender.

Britain soon had another new ally, the United States. In August Winston and President Franklin Roosevelt met secretly aboard ships anchored in Placentia Bay off the Newfoundland coast. Radio silence and Atlantic fogs gave the conference an unreal quality. Winston even had time to read historical novels and watch films every evening. He also busied himself with planning a joint church service, which he later recalled as "a great hour to live. Nearly half of those who sang were soon to die."

Although the conference established a warm personal friendship between the two men, as only the first of nine wartime meetings, its value was more symbolic than practical. The leaders issued a joint statement of principles that became known as the Atlantic Charter. It pledged mutual defense of the universal rights of freedom and thought both during and after the war and proposed the establishment of

*As wartime prime minister, Churchill inspired the public with his presence and his words. Here he is giving his famous "V-for-victory" sign outside Number Ten Downing.*

an international organization to guarantee secure borders and seas to all "States and peoples."

By the end of 1941 Britain and the United States were comrades in arms as well as allies on paper. After Japan attacked Pearl Harbor, Winston followed Roosevelt's declaration of war with one of his own. Even though it put Britain's Far Eastern possessions at great risk, Winston was glad to be allied with America. As a World War I colleague had said: "The United States is like a gigantic boiler. Once the fire is lighted under it, there is no limit to the power it can generate."

Winston was astonished, but relieved, when Hitler declared war on America shortly thereafter out of sympathy with Japan. Now four-fifths of the world would be fighting the dictators, and Europe would certainly receive its share of American power. Winston visited the United States at Christmastime to reaffirm those European commitments. Addressing Congress on the need for international unity, he disarmed his audience by starting his speech with the observation that "I cannot help reflecting that if my father had been American and my mother British, instead of the other way round, I might have got here on my own." He got a standing ovation.

A Grand Alliance of Great Britain, the United States, and the Soviet Union, forged in the closing days of 1941, marked the beginning of truly global planning and cooperation. Winston was almost constantly shuttling back and forth between Stalin and Roosevelt to discuss the African invasion, the European landing, and the development of the atomic bomb.

He also had to maintain goodwill among the three, a task that became increasingly difficult as the European invasion was postponed more and more. The Russians, who had been holding Hitler at bay since July 1941, desperately wanted the relief of a second front. Winston, who hoped to delay this action until the Allies were sure of sufficient troops, had to explain to Stalin why the armies were concentrating in the south rather than in the west of Europe. Sketching a picture of a crocodile for the Soviet leader, Winston demonstrated that with the available manpower it made far more sense to go for the beast's soft underbelly (the Mediterranean) than the snout (France). Stalin grudgingly agreed to wait.

The assault on the underbelly at North Africa began in the fall of 1942. Allied troops under the American General Dwight D. Eisenhower routed the Germans and Italians from Alexandria to Algiers. Britain rejoiced and rang church bells that had been silenced in case they had to serve as an invasion signal. Even Winston allowed himself some optimism. North Africa, he declared, was a turning point, "not . . . the beginning of the end but . . . perhaps the end of the beginning."

The liberation of Africa from the dictators' hands did not liberate those lands from British rule as well, however. Winston never thought to lessen the British presence anywhere in the Empire, war or no war. "I have not become the King's first minister in order to preside over the liquidation of the British Empire," he insisted. The Union Jack would still fly in Egypt.

His hard line on the Empire, as well as his openness with Parliament and the public, strengthened Winston's position at home. Polls showed that ninety-three percent of the people approved of his administration. The Conservative Party rewarded him by making him their leader. Winston was finally at the top of both his party and his country.

Things continued to improve for the Allies in 1943. Further success on the Russian and African fronts was capped by another conference. Stalin could not leave his embattled nation, but Winston and Roosevelt met again at Casablanca. There they enjoyed an odd mixture of business and pleasure. Meetings lasted only until five each afternoon. After that diplomats, field marshals, and admirals exchanged their uniforms for bathing suits and wandered down to the beach to play in the pebbles or build sand castles until dinner time. Even Winston relaxed and painted his only wartime picture, a scene of mosques and minarets, which he gave to Roosevelt.

They decided at Casablanca to defer the Allied invasion of Europe again in favor of stepping up the air war on Germany and beginning the attack on Sicily that would knock Italy out of the war. They also agreed that there could be no peace without unconditional surrender.

Stalin, who took the news of the delay badly, cheered up once the Sicilian operation began, for Hitler quickly diverted some of his soldiers from Russia to Italy. Winston suggested hitting Italy's knee as well as its toe, and the double punch scattered the armies of Italy's dictator Benito Mussolini and brought him into Allied hands. But German reinforcements made further progress difficult; in fact, Hitler's forces recaptured Mussolini and put him back in power in northern Italy. The campaign on the soft underbelly had met hard resistance, and any other ideas Winston had were dismissed as "all wishing and guessing" by the Americans.

The three men on whom the world's fate hung met together for the first time late that year in Teheran. They set a date for the European landing, and on the whole the conference was most cordial. Yet Winston was disturbed by the meeting. Plagued by his "Black Dog," his recurring fits of melancholic depression, he wondered if his strength would last the war and agonized over whether anyone had the right to send others to their deaths. He also felt left out. Three is always a crowd, even when those three are world leaders, and Stalin and Roosevelt had quickly established an easy camaraderie that often excluded Winston. It was at Teheran that Winston realized:

for the first time what a small nation we are. There I sat with the great Russian bear on one side of me, with paws outstretched, and on the other side the great American buffalo, and between the two sat the poor little English donkey who was the only one, the only one of the three, who knew the way home.

The Allies began their long-awaited push to regain Europe in January 1944 when they landed at Anzio on their way to

Rome. The Italian capital fell on June 4; two days later the Normandy invasion began. Four days after D-Day, Winston himself was on the beachheads, visiting France for the first time in four years.

Hitler sought revenge by dropping more bombs on Britain, but these were more of a nuisance than a peril for the people who had survived the Blitz. For all the increased fury on both sides, however, Winston was not convinced that the war would end quickly. In fact, he began to see an ever greater danger than Hitler: the Soviet Union. Alarmed by the Soviet take-over in Poland, he all but stopped talking about the Nazis and concentrated instead on the Communists.

To secure some balance of power in Europe, Winston journeyed to Moscow in October 1944 to negotiate with Stalin. During one of their talks, Winston slid a paper across the table on which he had written a list dividing the responsibility for the Balkan states for the duration of the war:

Rumania—Russia 90%, others 10%
Greece—Great Britain and U.S. 90%, Russia 10%
Yugoslavia and Hungary—50%–50%
Bulgaria—Russia 75%, others 25%

Poland was never mentioned.

Stalin studied the document for several minutes, then slowly made a big blue check with his pencil. Whatever second thoughts Winston may have had about delivering these nations to Russian care, it was too late to go back now. Russia had been offered almost a free hand in Eastern Europe to ensure at least some measure of British and American presence as well.

This situation was formalized at the Yalta Conference in February 1945. With Germany now in full retreat, the Grand Alliance met to set up the postwar world. It was a week of missed opportunities for peace. Stalin was too sure of his power to be willing to compromise. A sick and weary Roosevelt, unwilling to keep American troops in Europe any longer than necessary, made most of the concessions. Winston felt very much like the poor relation waiting for the crumbs his more powerful companions left on the bargaining table, yet he agreed to the proposals and compromises rather than lose any chance for peace at all.

Many things, such as Poland's borders, were not settled at Yalta, but some things were. Plans for the dismemberment of Germany and its payment of reparations were set. The three also endorsed the establishment of the United Nations, although there was some disagreement about which nations qualified as the great powers with veto privileges in the Security Council.

The Yalta Conference met in a war weary world looking for peace around the next corner. In March Winston spurred his people "forward on all wings of flame to final victory." But no one needed those speeches anymore. The war was dragging to its own conclusion.

Indeed, within a month, three of the leading actors in the struggle—Hitler, Mussolini, and Roosevelt—were dead; Allied armies had crossed the Rhine into Germany; and victory was at hand. On May 7 the Germans surrendered. The fighting that had claimed forty million lives came to an end.

Winston put away his battered suitcases. He suddenly felt tired. Relieved of the constant tension, the defiant lion of 1940 became an exhausted, querulous old man. The sixteen-hour days, the brandy, the cigars, the constant tension, and his sixty-nine years all rushed in on him at once. It would be a great relief now to turn all his energies simply to the affairs of the realm.

# ELDER
# STATESMAN

# 9

The coalition government had been in power nearly ten years, and Winston's cabinet five, when Germany surrendered. Winston knew he'd have to call a new election as soon as possible to see if he still had enough popular support to steer Britain through the rough waters of the Far Eastern war to a safe berth in a peaceful world.

To start the process, Winston resigned as prime minister on May 23. The king immediately asked him to head the caretaker government that would run the country until the new Parliament was chosen. Hoping to win an early election out of the people's sense of gladness and gratitude, Winston set the polling for July 5. Votes would be counted three weeks later to be sure of including the returns from British servicemen still all over the globe.

Winston threw himself into the campaign, traveling around the country in a specially outfitted train that let him perform his ministerial duties and still appear at meetings and rallies. Rather than proposing solutions to England's problems, his speeches attacked the Labour Party. In one broadcast he warned his listeners that a Labour government would quickly devolve into a repressive Socialist regime. "They would have to fall back on some form of Gestapo" to achieve their goals, he said, adding that it would be "no doubt very humanely directed in the first instance."

His words shocked the nation. How could their beloved war leader have turned into such a narrow-minded political hack? What had happened to his pleas for national unity? Compared to the prime minister's rantings, Labour's speeches sounded quite reasonable.

Afraid that his popularity was slipping, Winston grew increasingly worried about the election. He could not afford to let his mood affect his work, however, for that July he had to attend one of the most important conferences of the war. At Potsdam, in the Russian sector of a conquered and divided Germany, Winston met with Stalin and the new American president, Harry S. Truman.

This conference shaped the boundaries and behaviors of the world we know more than any other. Stalin's agenda included getting reparations, booty, and supplies from a broken Germany. Winston and Truman were more concerned with correcting certain breaches of the Yalta agreements in Eastern Europe. But whereas Winston wanted to challenge Stalin about such things as Russia's single-handed rearrangement of Poland's borders or the puppet regimes in the Balkan states, Truman chose to defer those questions to lower-ranking diplomats rather than risk any confrontation. Stalin interpreted this as indifference, and the indifference as tacit consent to continue his expansionist policies.

One very important decision did come out of Potsdam. During the conference Truman learned that the first atomic bomb had been successfully exploded in the New Mexican desert. He immediately informed Winston, who was thrilled and fascinated. He saw the bomb as one way of eliminating Russia from the world scene, for how could any nation without such a weapon consider itself a major power?

Truman, of course, had other plans for the bomb. Abiding by a 1943 Anglo-American agreement not to use the weapon without each other's consent, he asked for and got

Winston's approval to use it against the Japanese and bring the war to a rapid conclusion. The atomic age had begun, with all its terrifying possibilities.

Winston had to leave the conference early, on July 25, to return to England to await the election results. The night before the count he dined well and went to bed feeling quite optimistic. Just before dawn, however, he woke with a "sharp stab of almost physical pain" and a premonition that all was not going well. He fell back asleep and awoke a second time to sad faces and solemn news with his breakfast. By lunchtime the contest was over. The Conservatives had been washed out of office and the House of Commons by the Labour tide.

The decisiveness of the defeat stunned Winston. Bitterly declaring that he "did not wish to remain even for an hour responsible for their affairs," he resigned that night. And when Clementine tried to comfort him by observing that the defeat might be a blessing in disguise, her wounded husband snapped that "at the moment it seems quite effectively disguised."

Winston interpreted the election as a personal rejection and was terribly hurt. In truth, the people's wrath was directed not at him but at his party. They still remembered the prewar blunders that had left England so unprepared for Hitler. Voters also were expressing their disapproval of the negative tone of the campaign and their hopes of returning to a world where epic figures did not predominate.

Nor should the result have been entirely unexpected. Wartime polls and local by-elections had shown a strong swing toward Labour even while the country was almost unanimous in its approval of Winston. But since no one had read the writing on the wall, a wretched and miserable Winston Churchill again became a member of the Opposition.

Within a month, reeling from the double shock of America's atomic bombs and Russia's declaration of war, Japan surrendered. Deciding that with peace at hand his continued presence in the House was no longer essential, Winston took off on a long vacation on the Continent.

*Churchill, the elder statesman, arrives with President Harry Truman (far left) at Westminster College, where he delivered his famous "Iron Curtain" speech.*

It wasn't the rest he needed as much as the distraction. Winston was at loose ends out of office and frustrated by his sudden powerlessness. He turned down offers of honors and prizes from his own and other Allied nations because he "refused to be exhibited like a prize bull whose chief attraction is its past prowess." He also declined many invitations to lecture, preferring to sit gloomily in Parliament, sadly shaking his head over the new government's follies.

There was one offer he didn't turn down, however, and that was for a speaking tour of the United States. He took an extended leave from Parliament and came to America in February 1946, hoping to present his proposals for permanent peace to a more attentive audience. On March 5 he sat on the stage of an auditorium at Westminster College in Fulton, Missouri, listening to President Truman introduce him. He looked over his notes one last time, and then, when the applause died down, rose to begin one of the most explosive speeches of his career.

In simple, vivid words Winston pleaded for renewed Anglo-American ties, for the use of a United Nations peace-keeping force around the world, and, most important, for a strong and united policy against the Soviet Union. Using a phrase that he had first written to Truman a year before, Winston warned of growing Soviet influence and power:

> From Stettin in the Baltic to Trieste in the Adriatic, an iron curtain has descended across the continent. Behind that line lie all the capitals of the ancient states of Central and Eastern Europe. . . . The Communist parties, which were very small, . . . have been raised to preeminence and power far beyond their numbers and are seeking everywhere to obtain totalitarian control. Police government is prevailing in nearly every case, and so far, except in Czechoslovakia, there is no true democracy.

Winston's speech created quite a furor. Only six months after peace, and here he was talking about war with the Soviet

Union. Most of the world still saw Russia as an ally, not an enemy. Especially enraged, Stalin called Winston a warmonger and a racist. Why were the English-speaking nations , he asked, the only ones worthy of dominating the world?

Yet Winston's Iron Curtain speech did have its impact. Western nations reconsidered their attitudes and policies in the light of his warnings and began to try to avoid both further concessions to Stalin and extensions of those already made. East–West relations started to deteriorate. The cold war had begun.

Later that year Winston took his message to Europe. His theme there was European unity instead of division, and he stressed the need for building a "kind of United States of Europe" to enable millions "to regain the simple joys and hopes which make life worth living." Winston's proposal became the inspiration for America's Marshall Plan, which offered economic aid for Europe if those countries made a joint plan for its use, as well as for the Council of Europe, which brought several nations together for the first time in 1949.

For all the influence he might have had abroad, however, Winston could do nothing about the transformation of the British Empire into the British Commonwealth of independent nations. In 1947 he saw India and Pakistan join the world family, with all the conflict and bloodshed he had predicted. The following year he watched British troops return from Palestine and heard himself call for early formal recognition of the infant state of Israel. None of this activity pleased him. "It is with deep grief," he admitted, "that I watch the clattering down of the British Empire, with all its glories, and all the services it has rendered to mankind."

Life out of office was not all gloom and doom; it did have its compensations. Winston sold Chartwell to the National Trust, an agency that maintains many of Britain's landmarks, keeping the right to use it for his lifetime. Now rent- and care-free, Winston became a gentleman farmer, planting crops and breeding cattle.

He also returned to painting with all his old enthusiasm;

some of his pictures were even accepted and hung by the Royal Academy. And while age may have forced him to give up swimming and riding, he soon found a new sport to take their place—horse racing. Winston bought a horse, registered his father's old pink and chocolate colors in his own name, and thrilled to see his horse win several races.

His main occupation, however, was still writing. He wrote articles for *Life* magazine, and sold his World War II memoirs for more than a million dollars. Aided by friends, as well as several documents still in his hands, Winston set out to give the world his version of those grim years.

But none of these activities could deflect him from his real goal of getting back into office. Each local election since the late forties had brought more and more Conservatives back into the House, and finally, in 1951, they won a majority in the general election. Winston was prime minister once again.

He devoted this administration primarily to foreign affairs. Obsessed by his convictions that the great victories of 1945 had failed to bring peace, Winston strove to bring the former Grand Alliance back into accord. He pressed constantly for a summit meeting of the three nations, but was foiled again and again by American stubbornness, Russian political turmoil, and the tragic Korean War.

When England became the third atomic power in 1952 (after Russia had followed America into the arms race), Winston asked his staff to study its implications. The resulting Global Strategy Paper was the first document to suggest that future defense plans would have to be based more on nuclear deterrence than on conventional forces. To Winston this meant that all countries should be fully armed and constantly developing new weapons. Only by maintaining full military strength could any country hope to sustain the uneasy state of "peaceful coexistence" with Russia that seemed to be the best one could hope for in the postwar world.

The premiership took its toll on Winston. He was now nearly eighty, and while his health and vigor had seemed to return after his wartime series of colds, pneumonia, and minor heart attacks, each day now became more and more of a physical strain. One night in late June 1953 Winston was entertaining the Italian prime minister at dinner when he suddenly realized that he could not get up from the table. His guests thought he was drunk and discreetly left him alone. His doctors knew he had suffered a stroke, however. Although no word of this reached the public, the paralysis continued for several days. But the prime minister rested, and followed orders, and by August was walking unaided.

This was actually Winston's second stroke. His first had numbed his right side briefly while on vacation in 1949. Because he had recovered quickly, Winston had seen no need to change his habits. He continued to smoke, drink, and eat (at one point his small frame carried 210 pounds) with no thought of the consequences. But this second episode scared him enough that he began to think about reformation and even of resignation.

Better health brought better spirits, however, and retirement crept back into the dim future. How could he give up his power and position, anyway? What else was there for him to do? Yet some days he was willing to admit that he was tired. As he once told his doctor: "I feel like an aeroplane at the end of its flight, in the dusk, with the petrol running out, in search of a safe landing."

That November he reached his eightieth birthday, and all Parliament celebrated with him. Fellow M.P.s presented him with a large portrait of himself, which he didn't like, and he cut two three-foot-wide cakes to share with his colleagues. Presents poured in from around the world, and the nation drank to his health.

But now it really was time to go. On April 4, 1955, the young Queen Elizabeth dined with him at home, and monarch and minister toasted each other's future. At noon the next day he resigned his office. Returning home, he entertained his staff at a tea party, and then picked up his hat and walked out to his waiting car. As the *Times* reported: "Smoking a cigar, and greeting the crowd . . . with his famous V-sign, Sir Winston Churchill drove slowly away to the accompaniment of cheers and shouts of good wishes.''

Retirement was not absolute, of course. He kept his seat in Parliament, although he attended debates with less regularity, and soon took to showing up only on his birthday to receive his friends' congratulations. And he finished writing the multi-volume *History of the English-Speaking Peoples,* which he had begun planning before the war. Here in black and white was Winston's view of history, and it was all battles and great heroes. The American Civil War got more pages than the growth of the British Empire, and William Shakespeare was never mentioned at all. Historians called the work remote and static, a series of seemingly unrelated set pieces instead of a dynamic picture of the past, but the public was captivated by the book's prose and pageantry.

It was his last literary undertaking. Winston now had time on his hands, and it hung heavily. Contemplation of his honors—in 1953 he had received both the Order of the Garter and the Nobel Prize for Literature—brought him small comfort. Friends could not help, for most of them had died. Not even his family brought solace. Randolph, who had tried and failed many times to get into Parliament, was a political journalist and biographer, and twice-divorced. Sarah, who was an actress and who had by now survived three husbands, had been arrested many times for being drunk and disorderly. Diana had also divorced twice and would commit suicide in 1963. Only Mary seemed to cheer him with her five children. And Clementine, of course, who still sustained him after more than five decades of marriage.

Winston made his last visit to Parliament in July 1964. In his honor, the House unanimously moved to put on record its ''unbounded admiration and gratitude for his service to Parliament, to the nation, and to the world.'' Winston got up, bowed slightly, and walked through the chamber doors for the last time. Then he went home to wait.

He knew that death was near. Although he had once

been able to joke about it ("I am prepared to meet my Maker. But whether my Maker is prepared for the great ordeal of meeting me is another matter"), he now watched frightened and helpless, as all his faculties deserted him. He gave up reading, seldom spoke, and often did not recognize his visitors. All he could do was sit huddled in a big chair by the fire, staring into the flames, and giving it a stir with his stick when the room felt chilly. The world he had known and loved had gone. The Empire was ended, the aristocracy powerless. He alone remained.

On his ninetieth birthday he put on a specially made velvet siren suit and, supported by two nurses, appeared at his window to make the V-sign to the waiting crowd of well-wishers. He then retired to a champagne lunch in bed and reappeared at a small family dinner that night. Afterward he watched a specially produced television tribute to himself that incorporated most of his favorite music hall songs and sang along with the performers.

But by Christmas he was unaware of his visiting grandchildren. And one cold day in early January 1965 he refused his brandy and cigar. His doctors knew he'd had another stroke and that he didn't have much longer to wait. On January 24, the seventieth anniversary of his father's death, Winston died. His body lay in state in Westminster Hall so the nation could pay its respects. After a state funeral at St. Paul's Cathedral (at which "The Battle Hymn of the Republic" was played, according to Winston's wishes), the body was taken by boat down the Thames to the train that carried it to the little churchyard in Bladon where, finally, Winston came to rest next to his father.

On the floor of Westminster Abbey, near the Tomb of the Unknown Soldier, is a circular gray marble stone on which is simply written "Remember Winston Churchill." It seems an odd request. How could such a man be forgotten? For seventy years he was a leading actor in the theater of British history. He fought for the Empire, wrote of the victories, argued the policies, led the government. For many people, Winston Churchill was England.

His fame came really by chance; he could just as easily have died in comparative obscurity. The drive that propelled him to power by the age of thirty later sent him into the political wilderness, and many historians and biographers have argued that had he died in 1939 he would have been remembered as a failure.

For one thing, he was an anachronism. Winston was one of the last Victorians. He believed that the Empire was a positive force for law and order in the world and should never be dissolved. Never admitting that all people have the right to self-determination, he let the dreams and ideas of the nineteenth century determine his actions and opinions in the twentieth.

Winston also saw life as "a great Renaissance pageant." Heroic deeds and great men mattered most to him. His sympathies were naturally aristocratic in the age of the common man.

Lastly, Winston was a maverick. Independent, idiosyncratic, and imaginative, his colleagues and countrymen thought him incomprehensible and irresponsible. His unexpected ideas, eccentric views, grand risks, and flagrant self-advertisements baffled and exasperated his fellow members of Parliament. No party wanted him; no party trusted him. Winston was a man with a message, but nobody wanted to hear it.

Yet the very qualities that seemed to doom him to failure—his obsessive pride in England and its possessions, his historical preoccupation, his unpredictable imagination—made Winston great when World War II gave him his second chance. As his doctor recalled:

> He was indeed made for the hour. In the extraordinary circumstances of 1940, with the hopeless inequity of Germany and Britain—or so it seemed—we needed a very unreasonable man at the top. If

Winston had been a reasonable man he would not have taken the line he did; if he had been a man of sound judgment he might have considered it his duty to act differently. A sage would have been out of his element in 1940; we got instead another Joan of Arc.

"Another Joan of Arc." This was Winston's greatest gift to his nation and his world. For all his contributions to the shaping of *our* world—his acting as intermediary between the American and Russian superpowers, his building of European alliances, his constant calling for global planning—his most important role was that of savior of his country.

How did he do it? First by inspiring his people with his own unshakable faith in victory. In those 1940 speeches he touched people's hearts and minds, setting their fears at rest, answering their questions, sympathizing with their sorrows, and inviting them to help resist "the monstrous tyranny of that wicked man." He gave England pride, and he gave England faith.

He gave England a symbol, too. Winston turned himself into a character, a larger than life figure, a legend everyone could share. His cigar, his victory sign, his hats, and his siren suit became his trademarks. People would have missed them, just as they would have missed his silly mispronunciation of "Nazi." He was "Our Winnie."

Finally, he acted with great authority, almost putting himself above the law in order to protect the realm. "I had the sense of being used, however unworthy, in some appointed plan" to save his nation from the eternal shame of giving in to Hitler. His usurpation of power and his almost dictatorial direction of the government were in fact the heroic measures needed to meet England's supreme emergency.

But all his eloquence and courage would have counted for nothing without the spark of his irrepressible humanity. The hero who took time to make friends with birds and dogs, who loved to make a big fuss over his birthday, who preferred popular ditties to classical symphonies, who sometimes played jokes on his friends with a merry twinkle in his eye, and who was not afraid to weep in public made people in England, and all over the world, feel instinctively that he was one of them. By showing himself to be a man like any other, the old-fashioned aristocrat won the hearts of a great democracy and led it through its finest hour.

On his eightieth birthday Winston denied that he'd done so:

> I have never accepted what many people have kindly said—namely that I inspired the nation. Their will was resolute and remorseless, and it proved unconquerable. It fell to me to express it, and if I found the right words you must remember that I have always earned my living by my pen and by my tongue. It was the nation and the race dwelling all round the globe that had the lion's heart. I had the luck to be called upon to give the roar.

Winston's roar made all the difference and earned him his place in history. It also earned him the love and gratitude of his nation, and even today pilgrims to his grave may find there an anonymous bunch of handpicked flowers tied with kitchen string, bearing the simple, heartfelt message: "With grateful remembrance."

# FOR FURTHER READING

Berlin, Isaiah. "Winston Churchill in 1940," in *Personal Impressions.* Henry Hardy, ed. NP: Penguin Books, 1982.

Broad, Lewis. *Winston Churchill: The Years of Achievement.* New York: Hawthorn Books, 1963.

———. *Winston Churchill: The Years of Preparation.* New York: Hawthorn Books, 1958.

*Churchill, Winston. *A Roving Commission: My Early Life.* New York: Charles Scribner's Sons, 1930.

*Davenport, John, and Charles J. V. Murphy. *The Lives of Winston Churchill: A Close Up.* New York: Charles Scribner's Sons, 1945.

*Gilbert, Martin. *Churchill.* Garden City, N.Y.: Doubleday, 1980.

*Suitable for younger readers.

————. *Winston S. Churchill: The Stricken World*. Boston: Houghton Mifflin, 1975.

————. *Winston S. Churchill: The Challenge of War*. Boston: Houghton Mifflin, 1971.

James, Robert Rhodes. *Churchill: A Study in Failure, 1900–1939*. New York: World Publishing, 1970.

Lord Moran. *Winston Churchill: The Struggle for Survival*. London: Constable, 1966.

Morgan, Ted. *Churchill: Young Man in a Hurry, 1874–1915*. New York: Simon & Schuster, 1982.

Payne, Robert. *The Great Man*. New York: Coward McCann & Geoghegan, 1974.

Pelling, Henry. *Winston Churchill*. New York: Dutton, 1974.

*Wibberley, Leonard. *The Life of Winston Churchill*. New York: Farrar, Straus & Giroux, 1965.

# INDEX